Simulation and gaming
in education

371·36

27.

11.

12

Simulation and gaming in education

P. J. TANSEY
Senior Lecturer in Education, Bulmershe College of Education

and DERICK UNWIN
Senior Lecturer in New Media,
The Education Centre, New University of Ulster

Methuen Educational Ltd
LONDON · TORONTO · SYDNEY · WELLINGTON

First published 1969 by Methuen Educational Ltd
11 New Fetter Lane, London EC4
© *1969 by P. J. Tansey and Derick Unwin*

Printed in Great Britain by
Cox & Wyman Ltd
Fakenham, Norfolk
Hardbound edition SBN 423 41930 7
Paperback edition SBN 423 41940 4

Distributed in the USA by Barnes & Noble Inc

Contents

Preface

We are presently at a time of great educational change. Education is becoming child-centred rather than teacher-centred, and at the same time we are abandoning the ill-defined concept of intellectual excellence. Increasingly teachers, parents and politicians are coming to recognize that we can ill-afford to write off the young as failures on the basis of some abstract criterion of intelligence. The school should be a microcosm of society to which all its members have something to contribute.

This revolution in our approach to the school community is a result of many pressures. Significant among these has been the march of technology with its insistence on rigorously applied science and the quest for efficiency. Technology has at the same time thrown doubt on the traditional content and methods encountered in education, and introduced us to new and exciting methods for classroom use. One of these new methods is that of *simulation*, and the aim of this book is to introduce this and allied techniques to teachers.

There does not seem to be any level of education at which simulation cannot be used, but the authors especially commend the method to those teachers who work with the less academic school-leaver. The school leaving age is to be raised, giving rise to many reluctant pupils who will demand of their education during the extra year – and indeed before it – a relevance and interest which may have been missing from much of their previous school work. Our contention is that simulation is one method by which such needs may be successfully met.

Both before and during the writing of this book we have been very moved by the amount of help we received from people both here and in America. Of the latter Paul Twelker of the Oregon State System for Higher Education, Donald R. Cruickshank of the University of Tennessee, and Dale Garvey of the Kansas State Teachers College, Emporia, were among the many workers to whom we are indebted. In this country we have had help from those who could give it, and in particular from A. Aldrich, Wiltshire County Youth Officer, who allowed us to observe a simulation course in Salisbury. Seeing the outstanding results of this two-day course convinced us that the method was good and persuaded us to go on with its use in the training of teachers. We also owe a considerable debt to G. W. Geoghegan and G. Hatton of the Reading University Institute of Education Library, for their invaluable co-operation in obtaining many of the books and papers on which our work is based.

To all those who helped us, thank you.

P. J. Tansey
Bulmershe College of Education

Derick Unwin
New University of Ulster

CHAPTER ONE

Historical development

The first formal use made of simulation and gaming techniques in education was in America fewer than ten years ago, but the method is so old that its origin is uncertain. Let us briefly trace its history and development: a particularly useful exercise because it reveals an unusual relationship between education and business. It is the normal procedure for education to supply both the methods and the training for business, and indeed this vocational aspect of education is one of its terminal functions. In the case of gaming and simulation this process has been reversed, and education has taken from business a method which business in its turn had borrowed from military training.

DEVELOPMENT OF WAR GAMES

It is said that chess is the oldest form of war game, and that those tactical games that involve map manoeuvres have evolved from it over a long period. It is certainly true that early in its life, chess was used as a stylized, symbolic representation of war. This being so, the development of an instructional and of a planning element from chess and other games seems to be a logical development. These early war games were not played for pleasure alone. They did not consist of rows of toy soldiers faced by toy cannon, ready to drop at a shout. There were very definite rules setting out what the players could do, and what the consequences of their actions would be. Before very long the concept of abstraction had been developed also, and the pieces were not representational of soldiers, or ordnance. Thomas [5] describes a *'new Kriegspiel'* which was first played in 1798, and was the first game in which maps were used.

Towards the latter end of the nineteenth century, army games were divided into two broadly different kinds. The first, played to an elaborate code of rules, has been called the *rigid* war game. It reflects realistic situations, and the changing patterns of actual war were introduced by dice. Such games needed very careful and long drawn out preparation, and involved charts and tables to cover any eventuality which might be turned up by the dice. They were highly abstract, and were academic exercises. One could envisage their value as lying mainly in the direction of training in overall strategy. The second kind of games had an element of realism as their essential ingredient, and were played by large groups of military personnel in realistic situations, controlled more or less subjectively by umpires. Their value would seem to be on the tactical level and, as strategy and tactics go hand in hand in war, it is easy to see both the need and the reason for the parallel development of these two forms of war games.

The early games were Prussian, but they were quickly adapted and used by other countries. Captain Baring of the Royal Artillery introduced them into the British Army in 1872, and from there their use spread to the United States. Now, of course, they form a standard and essential part of the training of soldiers of almost every army in the world. In general the free play type of game is most often used because of its ease of organization, but the development of computers and their application to research in the armed forces has meant that rigid play games are easier to set up, calculations are quickly done and results are immediately available.

Military games had been played for well over two hundred

years before they were seen as being applicable to business and industry. From slow beginnings, however, such transition has become widespread.

DEVELOPMENT IN INDUSTRY

In an expanding economy, and in a period of rapid growth in company size, such as we have experienced to an increasing extent over the last half century, there arises axiomatically an increased need for staff at the managerial level. Companies may fill this need by enticing men away from other firms with offers of better pay or conditions, or they must initiate their own training programme. The former alternative does not solve the problems in these economic circumstances described above because the supply of able men, capable of doing the jobs adequately, does not keep pace with the demand. The need to take the second alternative of training their own men has been recognized by a large number of companies, many of which have had a management training division for many years. Lack of money, the perpetual blight of the formal education system, is not a worry for large companies. Their chief concern is with choosing adequate methods of training.

There are two methods. The first concentrates on the learning of facts, ideas and management skills by using the formalized activities of seminars, courses, and lectures which may be either internal, or conducted externally by outside agencies such as universities and business staff colleges. While these are valuable methods which are widely used in formal education, they have the disadvantage for people actively engaged in business that their message and information is conveyed only through the intellect. There is no opportunity of using this method of testing the learning on the job. The information that is given and acquired in such courses may not have immediate application, and so may be poorly remembered. The second training method is done within the plant by giving staff experience in different jobs, and by on-the-job coaching. This method of training is relatively slow and is restrictive in that it confines learning to a limited area. So we have the

3

broad based theory on the one hand counterbalanced by the slow and restricted methods of practical experience on the other.

Thus it was necessary to find a training technique that could incorporate what was good in both these methods and to weld them into one. The adaptation of war games to business was seen as a possible answer to the problem, and in 1956 the American Management Association developed what was in all probability the first business game. It was a competitive one suitable for general management personnel, and was called *top management decision simulation*. In it participants are allowed to act as executives, to make decisions, and to see the effects of these decisions. The AMA has continued to develop games which are used in conjunction with lectures and seminars in its courses to bring an air of reality to decision making, organization, planning and evaluation. Because of its historical interest it might be of value to describe this first game.

Before the game could be originated it was necessary to devise a mathematical model of the business world. For this purpose a number of formulae were developed in order to show the interaction of the decisions made by each competitor. These formulae or mathematical equations were then fed into an IBM 650 computer which was able to act as scorekeeper. The basis of the game was the division of the participants into five teams representing five companies selling identical products within the five to ten dollar price range. Phases of the game represented three month periods, and players were given a period of forty-five minutes to organize their companies, plan their strategies, elect officers, and draw up organizational flow sheets. They had to decide such things as the price they would charge for their product, short and long term budgets, and costs of production, marketing, development and expansion. They were given an initial budget, and decisions were made on a pre-printed form. These decisions were made by circling numbers on the form and these pieces of information were then punched on to cards and were fed into the computer. Not only the effects of the company's own decisions, but also the effects of those of its opposition were calculated and fed back

4

by the computer within a very short time, and new figures including balance sheets were then given to each company. Quantities sold, costs and profits were thus quickly available and the state of the company at the end of the 'quarter' was made known well within an hour of the start of the game.

The second phase started with an opportunity to review these facts and figures, after which they circled their new decisions in view of their changed state as companies, and after trying to guess the intention of their simulated business rivals. This was a typical business game in which several business years could be played through in the space of a few days. Feedback was effected by group discussions under a leader at the conclusion of the game. At this point it was possible to analyse points where errors of judgement, or mismanagement occurred. The value of the computer in this game was not that it made the game possible, because the game was not designed as a computer based one (the mathematical model was so simple that the calculations could be done on a desk calculator). Rather its value was that it made the exercise more realistic. Before the computer was used calculations took about three quarters of an hour to complete at each stage. After it was introduced they could be done in five minutes. This tended to keep the participants in their role, intent and interested, and as we will come to see later this is an essential element for success in simulation.

There is a whole theoretical basis on which business games, like bridge, chess and other games, can be analysed. This is the area known as game theory. It is believed that problems that occur in business can be solved by the methods of science: that is, by trying a series of well informed guesses and developing a system of mathematical analysis to fit the experimental results. Linear and dynamic programming are examples of specially developed mathematical theories. Clearly there are many problems in business so complex and with so many variables that a mathematical solution is impossible. Here management games and simulations play an important part. They are used to simplify the problem and to extract from it those essential features on which wise decision making hangs.

They depend, in competitive business games, on the establishment of models which are basically mathematical.

A simulation is an analogue, a reproduction of the reality, but the model upon which it is based need not be a mathematical one essentially. Indeed many of the most successful of the armed forces simulations were based on a physical model. Examples of this include the *Link Trainer* which was the simulated cockpit of an aircraft, and in this device many of the pilots of the Air Force learned to fly during the Second World War. For the first time, here is a simulation that is not competitive in the sense of one man competing directly against another so that there can be but one winner and several losers. Any competition here is between man and his simulated environment, and this is good because it is practical training, readily applicable to real life.

Because there is no element of competition with the Link Trainer there is no loser and hence no sense of being measured against one's peers and found wanting. In the Link Trainer mistakes could be made, and indeed frequently were made, without the censure or damage that would result from a similar mistake in real life. This freedom from censure permitted and even encouraged adventurous play, and enabled the trainee to measure what he *would* do against what he *could* do. What the trainee had learned he readily carried over to the 'on the job' situation, partly because he had become deeply involved in the training and partly because of the actual physical similarity between the training situation and the real life one. These physically modelled simulations have been developed and extended, notably to devices which simulate the interior of a motor car, and which are used for preliminary driving instruction. At the other end of the cost scale, the flight simulator for the Boeing 727 is a mammoth, complex affair that is alleged to have cost one and a half million dollars to build.

In this country at the moment, management games of both the competitive, computer based, mathematical types and the non-competitive, manual, simulation types (representing end points in a continuum) are in use, and some games contain a

6

measure of both. As far as participants are concerned the games are seen as pleasant experiences that cause a high degree of commitment and involvement. Students are highly motivated to learn by them, but few validation studies have been carried out. In one sense this is a good thing because we have an over-developed instinct for measurement. Thorndike's dictum that, 'If a thing exists, it exists in some amount, and if it exists in some amount it is measurable', can be a severe brake on progress. In another sense it is not a good thing because the theory must accordingly continue to be based on hunches. There comes a time when hunches must be proven or rejected before they become myths, jargon or commercial folklore. Pertinent questions exist to be answered, and on the answers rests the future value of gaming and simulation as techniques.

These questions are not of the kind which ask, 'Is this a better method of instruction than the classical course, talk, workshop, or seminar?' Rather they are of the kind that asks, 'What is the effect of competition in gaming?' 'Does it inhibit certain behaviour patterns?' 'Does it induce conservative patterns of behaviour and repress both inventiveness and experiment when both of these might be advantageous in a training situation?' 'Is there a transfer of training, and if there is, is the kind of training that is transferred the kind that we want to be accepted by our business administrators in the future?' It does not matter that the technique of simulation is measured against another method and found better or worse, for what teacher is there who has not felt, and felt often, the need for an alternative way of presenting information to a group of students who have failed to learn by other methods? These questions can only be answered by attempting to introduce the techniques of business in a place where the resources for assessment exist. One such place is the university.

Happily, simulations and games have begun to be developed in these places, and while there seems to be little indication that the questions have even been asked at this early stage, there is hope that the answers might be found there in the future. Taylor [4] at Sheffield, and several others including

Maddison at Glasgow, have applied the technique to academic learning in land use for town and regional planning. Following the work of Francis Hendricks who published the first urban planning game in 1960, and of Richard Duke of Michigan State University, two land use games have been developed and used in this country. Follow-up studies by Taylor indicated that students had enjoyed the games, had in the majority of cases understood the model, and also learned about urban growth and planning processes. Cautionary notes are sounded, but enough has been done to indicate possible paths of advancement for games and simulation, and to highlight the need for more information on the educational effectiveness of the techniques. It would, of course, be no bad thing to assess older methods equally critically!

The technique of simulation has become so important to the business world that a non-profit-making, international organization has been set up to devise new approaches to training, to popularize manager education, and to assemble information about similarities and differences in management and organizational behaviour in different countries. This organization, the European Research Group on Management (ERGOM) was formed at a conference in Barcelona in May 1966 and is financed by the Ford Foundation. ERGOM publishes a series of ten simulation games which deal with different aspects of management. Amongst these aspects are exercises on budgeting decisions, patterns of leadership, group organizational theory, communication systems, negotiating, and evaluation. Workshops are run for the training of people who are to conduct games in their own organizations, and these workshops yield data that when analysed can give information about differences in management and organizational behaviour, can form the basis for specific hypotheses, and can offer comparisons of methods from differing cultural settings.

The workshops are conducted in a carefully organized way. After the *introduction* to the facts necessary for the exercise there is *execution* of the tasks in small groups. This is followed by *analysis* and comparison of the results in plenary session. After a *study* of relevant literature the final stage is a *com-*

8

parison of the simulation experience with the participants' real life experience. The Research Director of this project is Dr. Bernard Bass of the University of Rochester, Rochester, New York, and two research co-ordinators are permanently employed at the European headquarters of ERGOM in Brussels.

DEVELOPMENT IN EDUCATION

The first published work about simulation in education refers to the project known as the *Jefferson Township School District* [2]. It has a close relationship to the business simulations from which it originated in so far as its first intention was to examine the 'on the job' behaviour of a sample of 232 elementary school principals. Specifically this study was designed to come to conclusions about administrative performance and personality traits of the participants. To this end a large number of articles of simulated material were prepared including a comprehensive survey of the school system: this was a real school system but its location was unspecified. There was a sociological study of the teaching staff of the simulated elementary school, information about class sizes, record cards, test results, school rules, and policy statements. Part of this information was carried on moving film, part on film slides, some on tape recordings and much of it was written. It took about five hours to read, see and listen to all this background information.

This background information is necessary in order that the participant can become thoroughly familiar with the simulated school system. From it he would know what had happened at parent-teacher meetings and school board meetings, and many other relevant things about the school. Each of the participants was put to work as the Principal of the simulated school, and was subsequently called upon to make the decisions relevant to that position. Here in this very first educational simulation we see emphasized a point which can be considered as axiomatic. It is the necessity to *assume* the role. A simulation cannot be effective if the participant is detached from the activity and is coolly academic in his outlook. It is the high degree of involvement that simulation induces that makes it an effective instructional tool.

When the participant is put to work as the Principal of the simulated school, he is confronted with a series of 'in-basket' items. By this is meant a number of problems which might arise during a school day: the 'in-basket' signifying that they need the attention of the participant. He must solve them, indicating his solution in writing. The essential feature about these problems was that they were real. They covered the whole range of conceptual, technical and human relations. They included marks of a student who was doing poorly in class, a report of a breakage by a child for which his parents would not pay, and letters from administrators who are part of the Principal's reference group. These 'in-basket' items were later discussed and responses compared by the participants.

Now, in the first place the intention of the exercise had been to find out just how elementary school principals behaved on the job, and when the exercise had been carried out an analysis of the responses was made. From these analyses, the 'normal' behaviour for each response was determined. This normative data permits subsequent clinical examination of 'on the job' behaviour in similar simulated situations, and permits the putting forward of a theory that simulation could be used either to replace the unsatisfactory technique of interview in appointments to various positions, or could be used in conjunction with it.

The *Jefferson Township* type of simulation was the first to be used in this country also. It is a method of training administrators in education and they occupy positions comparable to managers in industry. In our educational system headmasters enjoy a great deal of authority and freedom; they have great opportunities for doing good and tremendous potential to do harm. Not infrequently schools with good headmasters deteriorate under successors who are of the second class, and this decline takes very little time. Professor W. Taylor of Bristol University originated a series of courses for headmaster training while he was at Oxford University; latterly he has been assisted in this by Len Watson, a research fellow at Oxford. Their techniques include the 'in-basket' and are very reminiscent of the *Jefferson Township School District Simulation*. They have done a lot towards indicating the value of simulation as an instructional technique in this country.

Although the expressed purpose of the Jefferson simulation was to establish normative behaviour patterns, it soon became obvious that it had many other advantages to offer to education. It was seen that participants in the exercise became involved to a great degree. They did not just talk about how to solve the problems as is done in a case study; they actually solved them. They experienced fears, doubts, satisfaction; they became tired and frustrated, but most of all they became the person with the job to do and the problem to solve. This was obviously learning by doing. Many mistakes were made, but participants soon discovered that they could be made without any of the resultant consequences that would be disastrous on the job. In this sense the simulation behaves like the Link Trainer that permits the trainee pilot to land at minus three hundred feet without the expense of a funeral. Further it permits criticism and discussion of the behaviour that led to the mistake and allows other sets of actions to be discussed and analysed.

Additionally, problems can be presented that might not be reproduceable at will in a real life situation. These problems could be introduced against as much or as little background information as the controller of the game wished to give out. If, for instance, we wish to discuss with a number of headmasters the method of dealing with a petty thief we might have to wait for a long time before a petty theft actually happened in a school to which we had access. When the time came we would have to deal with it the best way we knew, and any mistakes we made could be held against us. In a simulated situation we can make a petty theft happen when we want it to, we can permit participants to handle it in their own way, and we can point out mistakes in joint discussion subsequently without anyone having to suffer. There is a further advantage in that we can be more experimental than is

11

possible in a real situation, for it is possible to stop the action or to build in checks that could not occur in a real life situation.

A further factor arising from the original simulation was that it was seen to be an *information supply system*. Concepts, research evidence, behaviour patterns and other material which is of use but which cannot always be made available in the real life situation can be offered and assimilated during the exercise. The participant in the simulation is ready for these concepts and information because he has been prepared for them. The problem has aroused his interest and he is ready to absorb information that will assist him with its solution.

How would we deal with a child who was rude, or always late, or told lies, or did not do his homework, or whose dress was not acceptable in school, or who was not working as well as we felt he might, or who could not get on with the music teacher, or who was a thief? You will say that it depends on the circumstances: simulation enables you to know the circumstances and the situation. The detail can be as rich as the designer wishes it to be and the scope can be as broad as is necessary. In simulated situations we do not talk about *children* but about a *child*, a child we know very well. We do not talk about *what might be* but about *what is*. We do not take dimensions and discuss each individually, but we see them and discuss them in their interrelated and dynamic interplay. And simulation lets us look at ourselves: it lets us do it much more objectively than ever we could in the real life situation when there is the compulsive need to justify our action against the criticism of our associates. We do not have to be defensive because in the end there is no criticism as simulation is a teaching device, and there is little personal threat.

Richard Wynn [8] quotes Marcel Proust in *Remembrance of Things Past* in which he says '. . . it is often simply from want of the creative spirit that we do not go to the full extent of suffering. And the most terrible reality brings us, with our suffering, the joy of a great discovery, because it merely gives a new and clear form to what we have long been ruminating without suspecting it.' He suggests that simulation offers the chance of replacing the vicarious, second-hand experiences with the

12

'terrible reality' in training of school administrators. In view of the discoveries made as a result of the first of the educational simulations, and of the accidental benefits secondary to the initial purpose, it is no wonder that the method has prospered.

The application of simulation to pre-service teacher training was first attempted in Oregon in 1961 when B. Y. Kersh [3] built a simulated classroom at the Center for Research on Teaching. By the use of multiple projection techniques, the class in this series of filmed sequences was made to appear as if it was reacting directly to the student who was taking part in the simulation. Several alternative feedback sequences were available for each problem, and the appropriate one was shown for each course of action that the student took. This feedback was a short film showing the pupil's predicted reactions and its purpose was to supply the trainee teacher with immediate knowledge of the effects of his actions, as in a real classroom.

In this simulation, which is unusual in so far as it is entirely filmed, the participant stands fairly close to a large central screen on which the film is projected. The size of the screen permits the image to be projected at life size. The simulations are mounted on three 16mm film projectors which are remotely controlled by the supervisor of the exercise from a hidden observation point. As he views the student's reaction he selects the appropriate sequence of films to be shown next.

Kersh [3] points out that the method is capable of further refinement, but indicates that it can, in its present form, be used by people engaged in both the pre-service, and the in-service training of teachers. In his view there are many problem sequences in educational films readily available at the moment, and although these were designed for other purposes, they would be suitable for use in simulated situations. He also points out that a rear projection screen is relatively cheap and that light control can be obtained by hanging curtains.

In Kersh's view, there are certain essential elements in the simulation technique. These essentials are that a suitable (filmed) stimulus situation be presented to the learner. That there should be a strong element of reality in the presented

13

situation so that the learner experiences the situation with a feeling of its fidelity. Finally he sees the necessity of the student being required to act out the response under supervision just as he would in a role-playing situation. Now, if use is made of film not designed for the purpose it seems likely to have two major faults. Firstly there would be no sense of continuity from one problem to the next, no sense of dealing with the same group as one normally does in a classroom, and so no feeling of belonging. It would be hard for a student not to become self-conscious under these circumstances. It would be difficult for him to assume the given role of 'Mr. Land,' class teacher. Secondly, it seems that an essential part of Kersh's simulation is the feedback routine, and this feedback must be missing if other than purpose-made films are used in the exercises, since suitable reinforcing (or remedial) sequences will not usually be available. It is probable that the Oregon simulation system has an important function in research, but it is not likely to be widely used in its present form as an instructional and training device because of its requirement of special skills and because of the expense involved in setting up such a workshop. It did pave the way for the use of simulation in teacher training, showing that it was useful. The first step is always the hardest one, and before long there were other experimenters in the field.

Cruickshank [1] and his associates at the University of Tennessee have created the fictional school district of *Munroe* and have determined thirty-two problems that have concerned first-year teachers in the past. In this simulation each of the participants has to assume the role of a first-year teacher who is teaching the fifth grade (eleven year olds) at Longacre Elementary School. As in the project for the training of school principals, 'Pat Taylor' is briefed in the background information of the community and of the school. Part of this information is simulated on film, filmstrips are used, and much of the information is written. When this material has been absorbed, the participant encounters the problems, some of which have been filmed, some of which occur as written incidents, and some of which are presented as role-playing incidents. This

14

seems to be the generally accepted technique in use at the moment and it has many advantages over the entirely filmed situation especially when money is not readily available. It is flexible, easily modified, less costly, and probably as efficient. Again, in this kind of situation problems need not be acted out alone, and so as a training technique it is better since it allows more people to be trained at one time, and larger numbers can be trained in any given time with less supervision using Cruickshank's methods than can be trained using Kersh's simulation.

In the classroom there is also an important part for simulation to play. The work that has been done so far seems to be capable of division into two broad categories. On the one hand classroom simulations and games have been used to train pupils in the acquisition of content and skills such as the manipulation of equations. On the other, there are a number of simulations designed rather to train people in social and moral concepts which are less specific than the first set. Layman E. Allen, whilst a law professor at Yale, developed a number of games designed to teach content of a mathematical kind, and to improve the logic of participants. These will be discussed more fully in a later part of this book. In general they are played with dice, are competitive, and are not simulations but games in the sense that bridge and poker are games. Amongst the second set of simulations and games that attempt to teach social and moral concepts are various 'International Games'. These may either employ real situations and nations or they may use hypothetical ones. The leader and pioneer in this later form is Northwestern University where Guetzkow, Alger and others have developed eight different simulations involving over five hundred students in just over two years. Other workers, including Coleman and Boocock, have developed and devised games at the Johns Hopkins University designed to give experience and training in social living. The element of simulation is much more highly developed in this division of classroom simulation than it is in the side developed by Allen, and while the element of competition exists it is not so greatly emphasized as it is in Allen's games.

More recently simulation has been used as a method of instruction in many different parts of education both in the UK and elsewhere. In this country one of the pioneers, Aldrich, the county youth adviser in Wiltshire, conducts regular week-end simulations designed to train youth leaders and their assistants. These follow the lines of the Cruickshank techniques fairly closely except that film is not used. Nor does Aldrich see any need for accurate representation of the physical environment: he achieves involvement in a different way. His students participate in an exercise such as planning a term's activities for a youth club, deciding on overall planning and then on itemized organization. Problems are concurrently introduced in a variety of ways, either written or in role-playing situations and act as distractions from what appears to be the main, time-consuming task of preparing the club activities for the next term. By using this distraction method, Aldrich ensures that there is little time or opportunity for his trainees to move outside their imposed roles of youth leaders. In his exercises it is fairly obvious that the role-playing activities are significant in the shaping of attitudes which are believed to be important. Observation of just one of these weekend courses has convinced the authors of the validity of the programme, and of its value as a training aid.

In Britain, simulation does not seem to have reached the classroom to any significant extent so far, and where it has appeared it has been topic-oriented. Walford [7] in London with several associates has devised geographic games based on the model of Cole and Smith of Nottingham University. Van der Eyken [6] has published the results of limited experiments conducted at Rosebury County Grammar School for Girls, with games of the international relations type. A modern history package based on the rise of Nazism in Germany in the early 1930s is being developed by Burrell at Bulmershe College of Education as part of the Schools Council sixth form general studies project.

Apart from these examples, a few others have come to the authors' attention, but the information given has been so diffuse that it is difficult to know whether they actually fall within the range of simulation at all. One of the difficulties that has hindered the spread of the method has been the lack of communication between teachers interested in simulation. A new method of information dissemination has come about due largely to the long delay in publication in technical journals. This is the method of 'pre-publication' in which mimeographed papers are circulated to initiates, and few outsiders learn of work that is going on.

One of the prime purposes of this present book is to make information about simulation available to a wider group of people who might wish to find alternative ways of presenting information and ideas, especially where traditional methods have obvious weaknesses or have been shown to be either unacceptable or to be difficult to employ. There are advantages which simulation has over more conservative methods of instruction, and these will be discussed in the next chapter.

BIBLIOGRAPHY

1. CRUICKSHANK, DONALD B.: *Simulation, New Direction in Teacher Preparation.* Phi Delta Kappan, 48, Sept. 1966, 23–24.
2. HEMPHILL, JOHN K., GRIFFITHS, DANIEL, E. *and* FREDERIKSEN, NORMAN: *Administrative Performance and Personality.* New York, Bureau of Publications, Teachers' College, Columbia University, 1962.
3. KERSH, BERT Y.: *The Classroom Simulator.* Journal of Teacher Education, 13, Mar. 1962, p. 110.
4. TAYLOR, JOHN L. *and* CARTER, K. R.: *Instructional Simulation of Urban Development, a Preliminary Report.* Town Planning Institute Journal, 53, Dec. 1967, 443–7.
5. THOMAS, CLAYTON J.: *The Genesis and Practice of Operational Gaming.* Proceedings of the First International Conference on Operational Research, Operations Research Society of America, Baltimore, 1957, p. 66.
6. VAN DER EYKEN, W.: *The Game is the Thing.* Times Educational Supplement, May 10, 1968, p. 1589.
7. WALFORD, REX: *Six Classroom Games for Use in Geography Teaching.* Twickenham, Maria Grey College of Education, 1968, Mimeo.

8. WYNN, RICHARD : *Simulation: Terrible Reality in the Preparation of School Administrators.* Phi Delta Kappan, 46, Dec. 1964, p. 173.

RELATED READING

CHERRYHOLMES, CLEO : *Developments in Simulation of International Relations in High School Teaching.* Phi Delta Kappan, 46, Jan. 1965, 227–31.

COHEN, KALMAN J. *and* RHENMAN, ERIC : *The Role of Management Games in Education and Research.* Management Science, 7, 1961, 131–66.

DILL, W. R., JACKSON, J. R. *and* SWEENEY, J. W. : *Proceedings of the Conference on Business Games as Teaching Devices.* New Orleans, Tulane University, April 26–28, 1961.

SHOUKSMITH, GEORGE : *Simulation and Industrial Selection.* Manpower and Applied Psychology, 1, 1968, 143–7.

CHAPTER TWO

The advantages of simulation and games

The basis of formal education in the schools of Britain and America has been the transmission of knowledge by the teacher to his pupils. This basis depends on the presupposition that the child is motivated to learn the content that it is felt essential for him to possess. His role in the past has been a passive one, and the expectation of those people who are concerned with him, his role set, has been that he will accept what he is taught and store it away until it can be related to his needs.

To assist him to do this, the schools offer him rewards for success. Some of these rewards tend to be artificial and take the form of marks, grades, and diplomas. Frequently these incentives result in information being learned for a specific purpose such as an examination and then quickly forgotten. It is now coming to be realized that learning is not an end in itself, but is rather the means by which the end is achieved. If the actual acquisition of knowledge were the goal for the majority, the relevance of what was learned would not be significant. But we do know that school children want to know the point of what they are learning, and recent reports on education such as the Newsom Report stress the need for relevance in the curriculum.

19

1966 Sprague and Shirts [13] have suggested that our goals for education should be to help people to become enthusiastic, to assist them in learning how to learn, and to provide them with the resources and aids which are necessary to further their opportunities to learn. Simulations and games are a great deal of use in the furtherance of these aims.

Coleman [5] has stated that the schools in America start the process of teaching from the assumption that the pupil is already motivated to learn. In this information-transmission concept of education the student performs certain actions in order to assimilate the material that he has to learn. The function of the simulation or game is to revise this model. In the ideal simulation situation the participant assimilates the information or material available to him in order that he may reach the goal set for him in the game. In this concept of education, action in an environment predetermined by the structure of the game results in a reward. This reward is not an artificial one. Given a goal, a student will seek information in order to achieve that goal, but it is doubtful if many students, given knowledge, will go out seeking goals or ways of using this knowledge. Coleman feels that winning is the most highly relevant goal, and so he has developed simulation games in which the element of competition is stressed.

There are others who do not stress the competitive element of simulation and games, although the majority of prepared school simulations in America do contain the element of competition. Those designed for the business world and for industrial training also make much of competition. Boocock [4], an associate of Coleman's, finds other values more relevant. She feels that by participating in a role-playing game, a participant will become more tolerant of those who play the role in real life.

She also says that simulations give the participant a feeling of efficacy, a feeling of being able to control the world around him, as opposed to a feeling of alienation from it. This is in keeping with Coleman's definition [5] on p. 68 of games '. . . Games may be regarded as a special invention in which children or adults practise with the components of life itself, a kind of play within the larger play of life itself.' If this is so, and if children can be shown that it is possible to control their environment within the structure of a simulation, then surely they will feel that it is worth making an effort to understand it, and as a consequence, their level of performance will improve.

Simulation does not have a universal application in education, but, in certain areas it is of great value. Apart from its use in schools, it is used in business for training at all levels from top executive to training for special operative skills. It is a useful research tool, has advantages over the interview as a means of selection, and is a highly motivating method. It might be as well to look at its use and its advantages in each of these fields in turn before finally tabulating its advantages.

In *business* and industry, simulation has been used for the last decade. In training it is held that simulation enables the broad company view to be passed on to the trainee in a different way from that which applies with the lecture method of training. In the latter, the weakness is that information is passed on only at the intellectual level. The trainee hears about the job, but does not participate in it. The content of his training passes to him not as a skill, as it does with simulation, but as a concept. The first of the business games was a competitive simulation, and subsequent game designers have tended to follow this pattern of competition. It is becoming more and more widely used in management training, and so its value must be seen, at least intuitively.

The competitive element has been less obvious when simulation has been used in the field of industrial relations. Here simulation of the role-playing kind is widely used. Its benefit is that a crisis situation in, say, labour relations can be set up and roles allocated. The participants can play the game without fear of censure if mistakes are made. Poor labour relations and wrong or unwise decisions on the shop floor result in strikes and walkouts. If this is the end result of a simulation it is all to the good. In the post-play analysis, actions can be discussed and alternative, wiser decisions reached. When the trainee takes his place in industry he will have a background of experience of on-the-job behaviour, and an awareness that his actions cause

21

reactions. This may give him the tolerance and confidence necessary to do his job more efficiently. Moreover, the mistakes he made in the simulation exercise will not have earned him the disapproval of his employers or the distrust of the men. Further, if we can persuade people in industry to assume roles other than their own in simulated situations, they will come to see the difficulties associated with those roles, and become more tolerant of the errors of others.

Craft and Stewart [4] state that simulation plays an important part in the sharpening of executive skills. In other words it is a means of teaching content. For them simulation has a threefold purpose. First, simulation makes it necessary to make sure of the facts; to collect, evaluate, and analyse the available information. Then there is an obligation to see the whole of the problem, or to diagnose the situation as it appears. Finally, it could be possible to find alternative situations for any given circumstance. This, of course, would be in the post-simulation stage. They place great emphasis on the post-play period, saying (p. 357) . . . 'However, the experience itself was not enough. Reflection, interpretation, and discussion were needed to crystallize it.'

This is, of course, the crux of the matter. The whole of simulation is merely a means to an end. It is an alternative strategy. If the lecture, or the case study, or any other method works there is no need for simulation. If, on the other hand, these methods are not achieving the results that are desired then it is as well to have an alternative method of presentation. Simulation is merely this method of presentation. It implies a structured situation which has been carefully prepared, followed by a simulation which may or may not be of a competitive nature, and finally the most important part, a critique after the game or simulation has been completed. Because of the dislike of post-mortems in most of us it could be that competitive games create a resistance in some people. It could well be that the game is the thing and that the result is final. If this is so, then competitive games, as opposed to group endeavours of the simulation kind, are not right for a number of people. The ultimate test is possibly the degree of involvement in simulation as compared with games with an inbuilt competitive element, and as compared with the lecture or case study techniques.

There is, of course, an area of business and industrial study where the value of simulation has never been in dispute. There was a need, and subsequently the search for suitable simulations was made. This is, of course, the part of industrial training where specific and complex skills have to be learned. If the task is difficult or dangerous, if the components of the task are complex and difficult to analyse, or if the equipment necessary for the skills to be practised is costly, or if the hazard to life or equipment is great, then simulated training is desirable or even necessary. Long before simulation had found its way into business training it had been used in the armed forces.

There is a research use for simulation in business education which has the advantage of reducing cost. When complicated equipment or processes have to be designed, as in defence systems or in some forms of processing, simulations are set up to investigate the operating conditions or to find which of several ways of proceeding or designing is most effective. These simulations are necessarily complex and commonly are computer based. In business training simulators have marked advantages where the cost of real equipment is high, where the degree of danger in training is high, or where the task to be learned is complex and when it is necessary to break down its complexity into separate skills for training purposes. Simulators may be used for training in either perceptual or manipulatory skills. They permit experience which has been gathered over a lifetime to be condensed into short training sessions.

Another research use for simulation is as a forecaster of future performance. When we engage in personnel selection we tend to rely on subjective evaluations such as interviews. The use of simulation permits the use of objective methods of decision making. As a preliminary part of the setting up of a simulation exercise which is designed to select personnel we would collect normative data from people who are on the job. This would be built into the simulation, and the performances

23

of the participants would then be compared with this normative data. Those people whose profiles most closely followed the normative data patterns could be selected for training. Wynn [15] states that an outstanding value of these simulations is that more candidates can be 'processed' in a given time.

Shouksmith [12] has used simulation for personnel selection in a wide range of activity from Lancashire cotton mill operative selection to the prediction of the suitability of Navy personnel for diver training in New Zealand. He has found items of two separate kinds useful. In the first, the essential parts of the job are simulated as described in his Mill Composite Dexterity Test (pp. 146–7). The second type of item calls for behaviour analogous to the activity being predicted. An example of this use might be in the selection of executive personnel such as managers or headmasters where the essential part of the job is in personal relations. Situations can be devised in which the applicant has to deal with typical on-the-job happenings. If the simulation had previously been applied to numbers of people who are thought to be performing the actual job satisfactorily normative values for the exercises would be available, and the candidate's responses could then be compared with these values. Very little work has been done in this area of simulation to date. Partly this is because of the difficulty in obtaining normative values, as the initial criterion of suitable, on-the-job performance tends to be subjective.

Simulation is useful as a device for the development of decision-making skills. Because it is a structured and programmed method, feedback can be built into a simulation and this enables the participant to benefit from the exercise in one of two ways. He can observe that the course of action that he embarked on in the exercise resulted in a desired result or pay-off which improved his position relative to that of other players. If this is so, then wise action is reinforced by the simulation. Alternatively, if the feedback shows that the course of action resulted in his being at a disadvantage relative to others, he will then have to make another decision to rectify these disadvantages. The advantage of simulation is that the participant is part of the situation, and is able to see the whole of the situation. He learns that his decisions depend on the whole of the situation and are best when full knowledge is taken into consideration.

Schild [11] says (p. 1) that the core of a game is to establish certain consequences (winning or losing) as contingent on certain behaviour (the play of the participant). This is, of course, true for simulation in any of its forms. Participation builds a high degree of motivation and gives a purpose to learning. Because of this the learning of facts and skills should be facilitated, even though it becomes a secondary function rather than a primary one as it is in normal, traditional methods of instruction. Simulation also supplies a number of contingencies in which success depends on certain behaviour patterns. The development of these behaviour patterns or skills is positively reinforced by success.

Simulation takes learning out of the area of abstraction and makes it a participatory skill. It involves learning by doing and this is of particular benefit where human reactions, interactions and emotions are involved. Skill is acquired through practice, and enables participants to learn facts, processes and alternative strategies. Abt [1] points out one further advantage of simulation in the acquisition of skills and knowledge. In real life there is normally a time lag between the making of a decision and the knowledge of the effects of that decision. There is also the possibility, in real life, of the making of costly mistakes. He indicates that simulation can provide a laboratory where experience can be gained and mistakes made. It can also accelerate training, and show the effects of decisions as quickly as it is desired to do so.

There are certain skills that can be taught only with difficulty. There is something about the skill of administration, or of selling, that cannot be defined and can only be learned by doing. But experience on the job may not be possible because it is too costly or because the trainee may be unsuitable for the job even after a long period of training. Learning by doing is an essential part of simulation and so it is an excellent way of both training and assessing in these complex and non-definable skills. Here it has advantages in time and cost over other training methods. A further advantage is that training may be organized so that each trainee is a member of a group; he then has to accustom himself to ideas of group loyalty, of persuasion, and of decisions jointly made as part of a team. This he can be told by conventional methods such as case studies, but simulation is the dynamic aspect of case study. Case studies are static teaching aids and are unalterable in the sense that history is unalterable.

While simulation has not been widely used in education in this country the need for it has existed in the past. It must not be thought of as an end in itself, but as a means of presenting certain material in limited areas of the school curriculum. As a technique it probably has more value at the moment in the secondary school than in the junior school, and may be best suited to that section of the age group that has not succeeded in the school system to which it has been accustomed. This larger group of under-achievers might be expected to include all of those children who are under-motivated, and for whom simulation should prove singularly effective.

All who write about simulation, anyone who has taken part in a simulation exercise, observers, all agree on one thing: simulation involves those who participate. It makes them enthusiastic and gives them motivation. Garvey [8] believes that the method can be used with any ability group, and reports (p. 14) that 93 per cent of one experimental population found simulation enjoyable. Attig [3] states that all of the reported inquiries concerning simulation and its effectiveness developed one finding in common: simulation is more enjoyable and more stimulating for the high school and junior high school student than are other techniques that have been evaluated in comparison with it. The type of simulation used most in American schools has an element of competition artificially built in. The tendency in this country to date is to leave the competitive element out of simulation. The competitive part of simulation causes a certain percentage of a population to dislike it. This could account for Garvey's 7 per cent who did not enjoy simulation. In the authors' experience in this country, no more than two per cent of participants have not enjoyed taking part.

26

Because few people can take part in a simulation exercise without becoming involved, it would probably have its greatest impact on that part of the school society which is under-motivated. A proportion of children, because of their environment, background, or parental attitudes find themselves out of step with the values of the school and so have little motivation to do well. For these children, simulation could be an important way of creating interest in the content that is deemed important by the school.

In the conventional classroom, a role strain exists for a teacher because he has to be both guide and judge. The guide leads his pupil along the paths of knowledge while the judge waits to evaluate and criticize. Simulation affects the social setting in which learning takes place by causing a shift of control. The role of teacher as judge or disciplinarian no longer exists when a simulation is in progress. There is no question of disciplinary problems. True, there is a lot of movement and a high level of talk on occasions, but there is no person who is constantly disrupting the class, for if he did this he would be interfering with his peers' enjoyment and they would not permit it. Nor does the teacher have to evaluate and declare a winner, for the winner is declared within the framework of the rules. Or there may be, on many occasions, no winner and all the teacher then needs to do is to lead the post-play discussion. This discussion should be lively after a simulation exercise because of the children's involvement in role and situation. The role of the teacher ought to be a very much less dominating one. The teacher should be less of a leader and more of a guide than is normally the case, and should fit into the background while the children proceed with their learning by doing.

While it is probable that simulation can be used with any age of children, it seems that at certain ages it is needed more than at others. It also seems that there are certain groups of children who need simulation techniques more than others do. The fifteen year old leavers have in their numbers representatives from each of the two groups above. A child leaves school because he is an under-achiever or because he is under-motivated. If we raise the school leaving age in 1973, these

27

children will have to stay on for a further year. If an attempt is
made to teach them in the classroom-oriented school they will
have an inbuilt resistance. But we do have to teach them.
We have to teach them things that they will have to know for
the future. One of the ways to do this is to bring the future
experience forward and to let the pupil participate in it now.
This is what simulation does. By involvement it permits the
significance of training for future expectations to be seen. It
provides a vicarious experience of a future situation or pattern
of behaviour. Simulations have been designed for a variety of
age ranges and many of them have proved to be effective.
They work well in the junior schools as well as in the senior
school. Teachers have suggested that, if the method were
better known and more often used, then we would have fewer
of the under-achieving, under-motivated at the top end of the
school waiting for the bell to ring for the last time and to free
them.

Little use is made of simulation in some of the subjects of
the curriculum. It seems to have more importance in the social
sciences than it has in the physical sciences. The games of
Allen and others that concern themselves with mathematics or
logic are exceptions, but nothing has been written to indicate
the amount of interest these games have generated in given
populations. They are not simulations, no role is played and
no vicarious experience is obtained from them. Allen [2] has
described them as 'autotelic' games '. . . that would help to
develop a favourable attitude among learners towards symbol-
manipulating activities, provide practice in abstract thinking,
and teach something about mathematical logic.' He also says
they were designed to be fun, and an activity that learners
would voluntarily spend time doing for its own sake. This is his
definition of autotelic. To this extent their value for those
members of a group who do not like mathematics is obvious.

In the social sciences, greater use has been made of simulation than in any other part of the curriculum of the school. The
social sciences are said to be difficult to teach because the
pupil does not experience a sense of belonging. He tends to
think of the past as dead, and of the content as not relevant to

28

his needs. It is postulated that simulation provides a structural framework with which to fix information in the memory. It is also argued that it provides a laboratory experience similar to the practical work that is carried out in the science laboratories of a school. Simulations in the social sciences have been carried out at all levels of education. In the junior schools they have been concerned with man's activities to make his survival possible. In the secondary schools and in higher education they have tended to try to make the student more acutely conscious of his environment, to make him less destructively critical, and to make him more tolerant of those who make decisions. They also have an important part to play in showing such things as how government works and how decisions are made.

In history teaching, simulation has tended to be directed towards international relationships. Guetzkow [9] and his associates at Northwestern University in America are pioneers in this field. They believe their simulation, called Inter-Nation Simulation to have heuristic value in clarifying theories of international relationships. People who play the simulation game play it as decision makers. They bring to the game their own characteristics as people, and their theories about how international relationships should be run. When the simulation is completed, appraisal shows where these characteristics and values need to be modified. Guetzkow [9] (p. 189) sees simulations as having value as research tools to test the various verbal theories of international relationships. He sees it as possible to investigate interactions and to establish models based on various theories and to test their effectiveness by simulating them.

Simulation can look at the large and complex pattern of human relationships and abstract therefrom parts that need investigation, or that are considered important. It can do this while training people as policy makers, or it can do so as a teaching aid, and as a complementary method to texts, lectures and seminars, in the teaching of international relations. For those engaged in training in foreign policy, Guetzkow sees two main advantages. He says that, by making explicit

29

what is implicit, it would encourage the use of more sophisticated procedures. It can also be arranged so that it contains a large number of critical situations and so can train for decision-making under pressure.

It is in the study of geography that simulation is most widely used in this country at the moment. It is used at University level in town planning and urban geography studies in general. In schools a number of enthusiasts such as Rex Walford of Maria Grey College of Education and Tony Crisp of Malory School have designed and used games that simulate geographic models. These games teach factual information, but they also shape outlooks and ideas. A game that was based on the railroads of America in the nineteenth century showed the players reasons why they were built. They had to make decisions in such a way as to strike the best balance between lowest cost of building the railroads and maximum demands for the services offered by them. They felt the chance hazards that the early railway pioneers knew because they were built into the game. These games not only teach the content efficiently because it has to be known before the game can be played, but they generate in the pupils an interest that is seldom seen in a classroom. In America, the HSGP [10] has used simulation game techniques in some of their units. They feel that these games make students see that their decisions can have an effect on their environment, that before decisions can be wisely made, adequate information is necessary. They also show that rational decisions are not always rewarded in real life, and they prepare students to accept the restrictions placed upon them by living in a community. In the social sciences, as in other areas where simulation has been used, it is not regarded as a substitute for other methods of teaching, but as a supplement to them. When used by competent and skilful teachers it is a most effective method of conveying fact and feeling.

Twelker [14], Cruickshank [7], in America, and the authors in England have applied the technique to the preparation of students in colleges of education. The college has a two-fold function in the preparation of teachers. It must supply the

teacher with an understanding of the basic sciences of education so that he can understand the theoretical basis for education as it is practised in his society. It must also give him the
practical basis that will enable the student to go into a classroom and teach. In general the colleges do each of these jobs
well. The difficulty that colleges tend to have is in preparing
students in such a way that they can bring their theoretical
knowledge to bear in specific situations as they occur in the
classroom. This is understandable for several reasons. It is very
difficult to obtain for the student as much experience of children
in a classroom as he or his tutor would want. This is because,
in the south of England, colleges are so closely grouped that
there are insufficient schools available in which students can
practise. If the student is in the classroom, there is no guarantee that the particular problem which the tutor wishes to
discuss will arise. What happens then is that the student who
leaves a college of education tends to be able to talk about
education, but has difficulty relating it to the classroom situation. His college experience has led him to see the classroom as
a place from which he is judged, and a place where the theory
he has learned has little relevance.

It is in order to bridge the gap between theory and practice,
the unnatural dichotomy of the colleges of education, that
simulation was introduced into training. The simulations so far
have been of the role play and in-basket kinds. They have been
found useful by students and have caused some tutors to
rethink their expectations of students. Simulation puts a
student into the role of the newly appointed teacher facing a
class. It makes him make decisions, and then allows discussion
of those decisions and the reasons why they were made.

Situations can be made to occur as frequently as they are
required in a simulation exercise, and so they concentrate the
experience of years into a limited training period. The method
is new in England, and few students have had experience of it.
Those who have, or a large majority of them, feel that simulation exercises have been beneficial to them. Amongst the
advantages seen by the students, the following have been
mentioned most frequently. Experience in the simulated

classroom gives the student confidence so that he knows what to expect when he is in the real classroom. The structuring of simulation enables him to recognize a problem or difficulty in the real classroom and to classify it. Each new problem is not a new experience but has a place in the network of past experience, and it is from this that both familiarity and confidence stem. Students can also make initial mistakes without censure. Having made the mistake, the student can discuss it with other members of the group without any loss of face, and it is then much less likely to occur in the real classroom. Simulation also enables a student to see that decisions made in the classroom have consequences outside it. Few of them seem to possess this knowledge as students at college before, or in the initial stages of, simulation exercises.

Simulation has also been used in the training of educational administrators on both sides of the Atlantic. In America it has been used to determine normative behaviour patterns so that simulation can be used as a predictive device. In this country, where little training is available for these most important jobs in education, use is made of in-basket techniques as a training aid. Trainees find it an exciting method of learning both course content and attitudes that are helpful in school administration and in dealing with the members of the administrator's role set.

Summarizing the advantages of simulation, it can be said that:

1. It motivates the participants.
2. It uses techniques of co-operation as opposed to competition.
3. It enables teaching for the long range future to take place even with pupils who are not highly motivated to learn.
4. It injects a feeling of realism and relevance into the classroom.
5. It enables complex problems to be made simpler and so to be more easily understood.
6. It changes the social conditions under which learning takes place. The teacher is less directly concerned with

administration of discipline and with her function as judge. There is a closer empathy between teacher and taught.

7. It is a structured or programmed presentation of information.
8. It has uses as a selective procedure.
9. Simulations can be prepared by the teacher, and so leave the control of the class in her hands.
10. Decision-making without censure is possible.

Simulation is a new technique and it may also have disadvantages. For instance it is very difficult to obtain quantitative evaluations of the effectiveness of simulations. This may be no bad thing, as we tend to be over-concerned with measurement in education, much of it of little benefit to either teacher or child. It is felt that the method has enough advantages to commend it to many teachers in certain stages and areas of education. If it motivates a child to the extent that he wants to come to school and enjoys the classroom experiences, that is measure enough for the teacher. The researcher will need to develop measures to tell him the obvious should he feel the need of them; the teacher will know already.

BIBLIOGRAPHY

1. ABT, CLARK C., *Twentieth Century Teaching Techniques,* reprinted from The Faculty, 30 (1), Aug. 1966, 13 pp.
2. ALLEN, LAYMAN E.: *Towards Autotelic Learning of Mathematical Logic.* Mathematics Teacher, 56, Jan. 1963, pp. 8–21.
3. ATTIG, JOHN C.: *The Use of Games as a Teaching Technique.* Social Studies, LVIII (1), Jan. 1967, pp. 25–29.
4. BOOCOCK, SARANE S.: *An Experimental Study of the Learning Effects of Two Games with Simulated Environments.* American Behavioral Scientist, 10 (2), Oct. 1966, pp. 8–16.
5. COLEMAN, JAMES S.: *Academic Games and Learning.* Proceedings of Invitation Conference on Testing Problems, 1967, pp. 67–75.
6. CRAFT, CLIFFORD J. *and* STEWART, LOIS A.: *Competitive Management Simulation.* Journal of Industrial Engineering, X (5), Sept.–Oct. 1959, pp. 355–63.

7. CRUICKSHANK, DONALD B.: *The Use of Simulation in Teacher Education: A Developing Phenomenon*. School of Education, University of Tennessee, Mimeo, undated, 8 pp.

8. GARVEY, DALE M.: *A Preliminary Evaluation of Simulation*. A paper presented at 46th Annual Meeting of the National Council for the Social Studies, Cleveland, Ohio, 23–26 Nov., 1966, Mimeo, 18 pp.

9. GUETZKOW, HAROLD: *A Use of Simulation in the Study of Inter-Nation Relations*. Behavioral Science, 4 (3), July 1959, pp. 183–91.

10. *The High School Geography Project*. Association of American Geographers, Washington, D.C., Newsletter, 15 May, 1968.

11. SCHILD, E. O.: *The Shaping of Strategies*. American Behavioral Scientist, 10 (3), Nov. 1966, pp. 1–7.

12. SHOUKSMITH, GEORGE: *Simulation and Industrial Selection*. Manpower and Applied Psychology, 1 (2), 1968, pp. 143–7.

13. SPRAGUE, H. T. *and* SHIRTS, R. GARY: *Exploring Classroom Uses of Simulation*. La Jolla, Calif., Western Behavioral Sciences Institute, Oct. 1966, Mimeo, 22 pp.

14. TWELKER, PAUL A: *Classroom Simulation and Teacher Preparation*. School Review, 75 (2), Summer 1967, pp. 197–204.

15. WYNN, RICHARD.: *Simulation: Terrible Reality in the Preparation of School Administrators*. Phi Delta Kappan, 46 (4), Dec. 1964, pp. 170–3.

FURTHER READING

BOOCOCK, S. S. *and* COLEMAN, J. S.: *Games and Simulated Environments in Learning*. Sociology of Education, 39 (3), Summer 1966, pp. 215–37.

COLEMAN, J. S.: *In Defense of Games*. American Behavioral Scientist, 10 (2), Oct. 1966, pp. 3–4.

DILL, W. R., JACKSON, J. R. *and* SWEENEY, J. W.: *Proceedings of the Conference on Business Games as Teaching Devices*. New Orleans, Tulane University, April 26–28, 1961.

MCKENNY, JAMES L. *and* DILL, W. R.: *Influences on Learning in Simulation Games*. American Behavioral Scientist, 10 (2), Oct. 1966, pp. 28–32.

CHAPTER THREE

Models and varieties of simulation

As the starting point in a discussion of models of simulated processes it is necessary to consider the limits or boundaries of the processes. This must be done in order that a theoretical basis of comparison of various types of simulation and game can be devised. There are certain questions that can serve us well here. The first of these is . . . 'to what extent is the simulation or game competitive?' Some have no element of competition in them at all while others are wholly of a competitive nature. Games such as chess, WFF'N PROOF, REAL NUMBERS, ON SETS, have as their essential common feature the fact that they are competitive: one person playing against the others in the game, or one team playing against another. The prime aim of players is to win, and to win is to be rewarded for so doing. At the other end of the scale there are simulations such as flow charts, weather maps, and wiring diagrams which are representational depictions of real life processes or conditions. In these there is no element of competition.

A second question that could be asked is . . . 'to what extent is the simulation or game structured or rule-governed?' Both ends of the continuum cited above are in fact structured, held in the grip of convention, and rule-bound. On the other hand it is a frequently used simulation technique to have a participant play a part. In such a role-play situation we leave him free to play the part in the way that he feels that it should be done. We make no attempt to direct him, and the process is unstructured. Thus gaming and simulation run the whole gamut of structure as well as of competition.

A third question of use to us is . . . 'to what extent is the simulation an active process calling for player activity to make it effective?' Now the playing of a game requires the player to participate. While *chess* (as an abstract conception) exists whatever happens, the *game* of chess exists only when participants are engaged in the playing of the game. It is also true to say the dramatic experience of role-playing calls for active participation on the part of the player. In both of these aspects of simulation then the active element of participation is a dominant and essential feature. At the other end of the scale the pure simulations of weather map, bar graph, and wiring diagrams require no participation. They are singularly passive devices.

We thus have three characteristics which can be used to describe any simulated process:

    i *the degree of competition,*

    ii *the degree of structure,*

    iii *the degree of participation.*

Each of these factors can vary between zero and some theoretical maximum, so they may be regarded as three *dimensions* of simulation and any simulation or game could be characterized by the values of these dimensions.

Simulation is often described as a process involving the use of a *model*. It will be helpful now to specify what we mean by the term model. A model is an abstraction of things held to be important in the real life situation. It should state or show the functional relationship between variables, and be designed so that an investigator can look at an aspect of a naturally occurring complex situation without becoming confused by the complexity of it. In this case, the model would indicate only those parts of the real life situation that were believed to be important. The model may be logical, mathematical or symbolic. It may have rigidly defined limits or it may be loosely constructed. Abt Associates [1] say that the merits of a model may be estimated according to . . .

1. *Validity.* How truly representative of the real life situation is the model?
2. *Coverage.* How much of what is important in the real life situation is present in the model?
3. *Comprehensibility.* How easy is the model to understand and conversely how easily are the significant processes which have been modelled understood from the model?
4. *Experimental Utility.* How useful is the model in permitting the experimental manipulation of the real life processes in order that they may be investigated in changing conditions and under differing circumstances?
5. *Applicability.* Is the model significant in so far as it assists in the understanding and possibly in the control of the real life conditions that are depicted by it?

These seem to be far more valid criteria on which to base the effectiveness of a simulation exercise than those evaluative criteria that try to establish that it is a better method of learning or of teaching than any other method. A thing may very well be good in its own right without having to be better than some other thing. We readily accept that the doctor and dustman both perform useful functions in the community and that each may be better than the other in a certain field of interest. One can fix your septic tank while the other is fixing your septic finger. If the problem as to which was of the most use was posed, the answer would have to be that it depended on the needs of the moment. All that can be said at this stage about the comparative virtues of simulation exercises is that they work under certain conditions and they help certain learners.

One mistake when programmed learning was introduced was that it was made to appear as a competitive learning technique in the behaviourist mould. From this other mistakes followed as a logical sequence: the invented jargon understood by only the initiates, the changing attitudes as time passed about such things as positive reinforcement and its possible role in the complex processes of human learning, the attendant teaching machines trying to make sure of their share on pay day, and inevitably, the consequential minimal effect on formal education for the majority of teachers and pupils in British schools. It is essential that no exaggerated claims be made for simulation, and that teachers are permitted to test it and judge for themselves. It is important that we do not make it dependent on machinery, nor price it out of the range of schools; this would be easy to do if we were interested only in spectacle. And it is desirable that it should become a method without an 'in-language' which needs an official translator before it can be understood.

Models for simulations can be arranged with ease by teachers at a cost that can be met by any school that has duplicating facilities and a stock of paper. Teachers are busy people, of course, and the continual contact in the classroom may make them unwilling to spend long hours in the evening inventing exercises for their classes. It is here that publishers can help. Small pamphlets must be prepared cheaply so that teachers can afford them. Spirit duplicator masters could be made available for teachers who wish to reproduce information sheets, and teachers would then test and evaluate the method. It could then perform a useful job in certain circumstances as another way to try to teach, a way that is novel and interesting, useful and motivational.

There is of course something to be said for jargon, because, if a new method is presented without it then it may seem so simple or so insignificant that people interested in the same areas may miss it altogether. After all, *simulation* used in this context is a jargon word in that it was devised by somebody at some time. Who was responsible for it, or when, is no longer certain but it is sure that somewhere it fired the imagination and persuaded people to develop a technique. The word was not the deed however because the action came before simulation appeared anywhere except in the *Oxford Dictionary*. In 1950 Jacobs [3] talked of *sociodrama*, and was already a

long way towards describing simulation. But he gets no credit
that is immediately apparent in the literature, and the historical descriptions of simulation *qua* simulation do not include
anything educational before 1959. True, Jacobs presented no
rationale for what he was doing and, true, his work was drama
based, but it was a beginning. It might be as well to take
a look at the development of the technique from the time
that the game was named, and see if we can find a model,
no matter how loosely formed in the early work. It might
be possible then to see to what extent current opinion shares
the views of the early workers in the field once it had been
named.

The model used in the 'Jefferson County' simulation hinged
on the '*in-basket*' technique. This is a type of presentation in
which the problems to be solved are written and offered in a
form similar to the way they might appear in the in-basket of
a Principal in a normal school. The items are selected in such a
way that they represent typical administrative problems, and
it is hoped that because they are presented under controlled
conditions the answers given to them permit analysis of the
behaviour of the participant. The control comes about in the
main by the design of the situation in which the in-basket
problems are set. The originator of the exercise can devise a
situation, and can then build a background to it, supply
additional material to the simulation participant, and thus
exert control. An in-basket problem must be realistic, in so far
as it should be typical of the problems that a participant in
the simulation might have to face at any time. In general the
problems must be significant ones dealing with an aspect of the
participant's job or a clear area in which it is thought desirable
that instruction is needed or should be given.

Before in-basket techniques can be effective, a certain
amount of preparation is essential. The originator of the
simulation must begin by asking, 'what is important in the
situation which I am trying to illustrate?' Analysis is the key
to success if this kind of method is to be used. It will be necessary to ask what is important in the situation that is to be
simulated, and, of course, to ask which aspects of a given

39

situation should be stressed. For example the general background and theory of an operation may be well known but there may also be a bottleneck or a bar at a certain point, and it could possibly be that greater efficiency could result if this bar was recognized. Now if the originator knows what the blocks are it is easy to illustrate them. It then becomes necessary to compile background information based on the real life situation, and to utilize this information to build up the problem. The participant is then required to evaluate the information and to apply his skill and previous training or experience in order that he may offer a solution to the problem that has been posed. In-basket techniques extend case studies to a practical level.

The in-basket problem and its subsequent solution may be made use of in either of two ways. First, we may require the learner to understand behaviour patterns or modes of operation in certain particular cases where information is not readily available. In this method of use the in-basket is a more valid method than the questionnaire because it calls for decisions while the participant is actually in the 'on-the-job' situation. He is committed and his reactions are liable to be spontaneous and neutral. If the same information was asked in a questionnaire replies might be less than honest because of the tendency to try to answer questions in the way that is most likely to accord with the questioners' presumed requirements. If a teacher is asked on a television interview whether he believes in corporal punishment he might say that he does not, but the same teacher may well have struck a boy at some time, and may do so again. In the abstract he perhaps believes that corporal punishment is undignified, but he may also recognize situations where he believes it to be necessary. Let us suppose that one of these circumstances was *dishonesty*. We could supply the relevant background information for an in-basket simulated situation on this topic and ask a statistically relevant number of teachers to react to the problem as part of a simulation. Because of their involvement the probability is that their reactions would be natural, not artificial. By analysing their solutions it is possible to find what the average teacher might do in these circumstances, and also the percentages of teachers who would react in different ways.

An in-basket item that would be suitable for this situation might contain the following items:

ITEM 1. BACKGROUND INFORMATION

Tony Pomfrit, aged fourteen is one of a pair of twins in the C stream of the fourth year in the Coronation Street Secondary Modern School where you are an assistant teacher teaching mathematics. You have never actually taught this boy, but know him quite well. He is a fluent lad, presentable, and has a great flair for selling tickets for the school fair. Last year he sold £7 10s. 0d. worth, beating the next best seller by over £4. His father is a member of the Armed Forces and is seldom at home. He lives with his grandmother who is a strict disciplinarian. He is quite a likeable boy who has been in the usual sort of school trouble for not doing work, smoking in the toilets and so on. He is no leader, but is not unpopular either with staff or with boys.

ITEM 2. SITUATION

On Thursday, 6th June, you call into the Queen Victoria public house, where you are well known. The manager asks you why you do not take your Mackeson bottles back to the off-licence where you bought them, as he knows that you have not bought bottles of this stout at his hotel. Subsequent questioning leads to the discovery that a lad has brought in two dozen empty bottles together with a note signed with your name asking that he be given the money for them. The manager did so as a favour to you. You have reason to believe that the lad who did this was Tony Pomfrit, and subsequent questioning at school leads to an admission of guilt by the boy.

How are you going to deal with the situation?

Suppose that this problem was presented to a hundred teachers and their replies were analysed, the following pattern might emerge. (Presuming that each participant could give more than one reply.)

Talk to the boy	74
Report to the headmaster	86
Notify boy's parents	12
Cane the boy	27
Do nothing	6
Find out if he needed the money	4
Find out where he got the bottles	1
Compel him to make restitution	1
Call in the police	1
Ask for a psychologist's report	1

213 answers

From the replies to this question it is clear that the average teacher in these circumstances would first of all talk to the boy and then would hand the matter over to the headmaster in order that he could deal with it.

The experienced teacher reading this book will say that this has merely served to underline the things he knew already. He will feel that too much effort has been made to establish a normative pattern that he could have told the originator of the in-basket before he started, thus leaving him free to do something useful. The experienced teacher will also say that it is an unlikely situation. However, it is a situation that has occurred, and one which poses valid questions to the parties involved.

There is another side to this picture. How did the reader get his present job? By interview almost certainly if he is a teacher. And what about the jobs he has failed to get by interview? And what about the large number of incompetents who get jobs by interview in every walk of life, and who subsequently prove to be incapable once they have been appointed and when nothing can be done about it? How many teachers carry other teachers' discipline for them, or try to balance their registers at the end of term, and was there ever a child who suffered through a bad teacher (or a student through a bad lecturer) who had been appointed after a searching interview? Surely common experience suggests that the technique of interviewing is unsatisfactory and inefficient. If this is so then simulation, of which in-basket techniques are a part, might offer a more scientific alternative. The method can be used in the way that has been illustrated above to determine normative approaches to situations which are typical of the classroom and school situation. It may be said that the above situation was hardly typical, but no one would deny that theft and dishonesty are commonplace. Now, if an in-basket is built up of enough separate items to test applicants in all the areas of teacher competence that are believed to be significant, a very good profile of the person will emerge. His weaknesses and strengths will be highlighted.

Having determined normative values for each separate item in the in-basket a further technique can be used to make the task of investigating responses easier. This is the method of 'weighted scores' in which a value is given to each response. Those nearest the norm would have the highest value. To determine the weighted score the following procedure is adopted. Taking the example above, there were a hundred participants and there were two hundred and thirteen responses to the problem. Divide the number of participants by the number of responses; in this case $\frac{100}{213} = \cdot47$. Now multiply the number of responses to each figure by this weighting to get the 'weighted score'. The 'weighted score' for the response 'talk to the boy', would be $74 \times \cdot47 = 34\cdot78$. In an in-basket exercise, the candidate with the highest 'weighted score' would be the one whose behaviour most closely followed the normative pattern.

There are defects in the scheme. It might be possible for applicants for jobs to acquire a 'simulation technique' as some have developed an 'interview technique' at present. As long as the problems are left open-ended and alternative solutions are not indicated on the response sheet, this possibility is reduced. In any case it can be used in conjunction with interviews, and

43

may indeed form a basis for the questions asked by the interviewing panel.

Having discussed the use of simulations in general, and in-basket techniques in particular, as normative value determinants, it is appropriate to turn to their second use as *training techniques*. It is here that their value to the schools lies. There can be no doubt in the mind of anyone who has used the methods of simulation that they are highly motivating and that they produce a great deal of involvement on the part of the participants. These are ideal conditions for learning to take place. If we present what we want to be learned, discussed, or felt in the form of a simulation it might be much more acceptable, especially to older pupils, than formal classroom methods. In the traditional formal classroom structure can be seen much that is different from real life. Children are in competition with each other, there is one winner and there are several losers. But this is not so in real life: there does not have to be a loser for each winner, people are not always in competition, and indeed one of the essentials of society is that people do in fact work together. Possibly then, simulation with its group-working in which participants work co-operatively, and in which there *need* be no personal winner, brings the classroom nearer to life than do conventional methods.

The original theoretical basis on which simulation as a means of instruction and training was based was the 'operant conditioning model' of Bert Y. Kersh [4] of the Oregon State System of Higher Education Teacher Research Division. This is in direct line with the behaviourist theory on which Skinner's programmed learning techniques were based. It was presumed that the behaviour patterns of student teachers on teaching practice were due to stimuli that occurred within the classroom. Thus, the student teacher performed a teaching action and observed its effects on his pupils. These effects acted as reinforcers, either positive or negative, and shaped the student's further actions in teaching. If this theory was accepted, the next logical step in the argument would be that lectures, seminars, 'principles of education' courses and 'method' courses that the student attended in college helped him to be

44

articulate, to talk about teaching, but only classroom experience could actually help him to teach. This is a view still widely held by practising teachers in this country. Such teachers are the ones who tell a new teacher to forget all he has been told at college, and to start *really* to learn from the front line practical teachers who are actually doing the job. Now Kersh argued that if a method were found that would allow the supervising tutor to control the events that took place in the classroom the behaviour of the student teacher could be effectively shaped by the reinforcing of acceptable behaviour patterns, or successive approximations to them. Simulation was seen as such a method.

Using this theoretical model, Kersh developed a simulated classroom which he called Mr. Land's Sixth Grade. As an aside, both the Jefferson County simulation and that used by Cruickshank at Tennessee have given a name to the central participant so that it can be either a man or a woman. This is an important consideration, for in the early work carried out by the authors, women students protested at the difficulty of having to assume the identity of a male teacher in a simulation exercise. In this simulated classroom Kersh tried to introduce the idea of a feedback that is controlled by the participant. In his earlier work this feedback was intended to act as a reinforcing stimulus, but as it has developed the stimulus may or may not be positively reinforcing. If the student's reaction to a situation is so unusual, or so wrong, that it is difficult to reinforce his behaviour positively then the possible consequences of his actions are shown to him, and the feedback is now regarded merely as being informative, and a part of the continuing process of instruction. In the American jargon, such a method of using simulation is known as an 'information-system approach', as postulated by Ryans [5]. The work of Kersh and of Cruickshank, and the Jefferson County Simulation, are more fully described in Chapter 7.

Methods of presentation of simulations are many and varied. Apart from the in-basket techniques that have been discussed in the earlier part of this chapter, a method that is widely used is that of *role-play*. In this the participant has to assume

45

the role of some other person. Thus the pre-service trainee teacher may have to assume the role of a new teacher in a classroom, and deal with the difficulties as they arise in the simulated situation, or the child in the classroom may have to assume the part of a middle-class merchant in eighteenth-century England, and so on according to the topic of study. In role-play situations the participant actually attempts to *be* the person whose role he has taken on. It is no use asking him the question, 'What would you do *if* you were a merchant in eighteenth-century England and . . .' No, he must be given enough information to fill the role adequately and then told 'You *are* an eighteenth-century merchant and ... has happened, what are you going to do about it ?' One of the things that has not been determined is how important realism is in these role-plays. In the authors' experience it does not seem to be necessarily of great importance, but what *is* very important is *involvement* in the role. This can be achieved by introducing an element of realism it is true. It can also be achieved by making the participant commit himself to the role.

The authors have involved participants by supplying a continuing task, in this case preparing a lesson plan, and while the students were engaged in doing this, injecting a variety of crisis situations which required their immediate attention. This method has also been used very effectively in the training of youth leaders in Wiltshire by Aldrich [2] the County Youth Officer. He sets as a continuing problem the arranging of a programme for a term in a simulated youth club. His injected problems are both in-basket and conveyed by visitors assuming the roles of interested outsiders whose existence modifies the pattern of activity of the youth club. His trainees work in groups and reach group decisions. Very probably, group structure is highly significant in these conditions; it is astonishing to see how behaviour patterns have been modified and shaped by just one week-end of such simulation activity.

Film might be used to advantage to present background material, even if a complete Kersh-style system is too expensive. For instance a film of the locality of the school, and of the home of a pupil whose behaviour pattern and actions were to be simulated would be most useful if a classroom situation was to be simulated for pre-service teachers. Tape recordings of interviews and meetings are also useful scene-setters, and as closed circuit television becomes more common, it will be used more and more in this field. Still and cine film, drawings, plans, and role plays can all be put on to closed circuit television to give continuity, and high quality production. There is a tendency, however, to use this medium unwisely, because of the very flexibility and convenience of CCTV. It is only too easy to include a formidable array of visual techniques, and this not infrequently leads to a mish-mash of teaching fragments, confusing to eye, ear and brain. Media should be used as dictated by appropriateness and tempered by necessity. All this adds up to the fact that the medium in which a simulation is presented is probably not of overriding importance. What is of greater importance is the preparation of the model.

There are a number of decisions to be made by a person wishing to set up a simulation, and listing these might be a suitable way to end this chapter.

1. Decide what you expect of the simulation, i.e. what you expect it to do. It could for instance teach facts, bring out beliefs which you as a teacher believe to be valuable, beliefs of a social or of a moral nature; it could test attitudes, or it could be used as a means of selecting personnel.

2. Within this overall pattern of expectation settle the broad planning. How many classroom hours do you expect the simulation to occupy? How can all the characters being portrayed and all the participants be kept fully occupied during the course of the simulation? What setting is to be used for it? What background knowledge must be given? How many participants must be catered for?

3. At this stage the detail can be filled in. Decisions will have to be made about the roles that individuals play, about ways of decision making (group or individual or a combination of both), and about feedback methods.

4. Specify each participant's aims and objectives (wealth, escape from punishment, advantage, power, exertion of influence over others), and where necessary his resources (physical appearance, social background, moral attitudes, wealth, political associations, and the knowledge he possesses).

5. By this stage the simulation will be taking shape, and although the form is not yet certain much of the hardest work has been done. What is left to be decided are the rules of play, which do not need to be formally delineated in a simulation.

It takes very little experience to originate a simulation, and after a brief initial period the steps outlined above will be carried out intuitively.

There has been no discussion in this chapter of games, the competitive element of simulation. A separate chapter has been allocated to the topic of games and to a brief look at the theory behind them.

BIBLIOGRAPHY

1. ABT ASSOCIATES INC.: *Report of a Survey of the State of the Art: Social, Political and Economic Models and Simulations.* Cambridge, Mass., Abt Associates Inc., Nov. 1965, p. 67 *et seq.*

2. ALDRICH, A. A.: *Nonsuch Youth Club.* Trowbridge, Wiltshire Training Agency. Undated, mimeo.

3. JACOBS, ARTHUR J.: *Sociodrama and Teacher Education.* Journal of Teacher Education, 1, 1950, 193–8.

4. KERSH, B. Y.: *The Classroom Simulator.* Journal of Teacher Education, 13, Mar. 1962, 110–11.

5. RYANS, D. G.: *An Information-System Approach to Theory of Instruction, with Special Reference to the Teacher.* System Development Corporation, SP–1079, 1963.

RELATED READING

ATTIG, JOHN C.: *The Use of Games as a Teaching Technique.* Social Studies, 58, Jan. 1967, 25–29.

Models and varieties of simulation

HERSHEY, GERALD L., KRUMBOLTZ, JOHN D. *and* SHEPARD, LORRAINE V.: *Effectiveness of Classroom Observation and Simulated Teaching in Introductory Educational Psychology Course.* Journal of Educational Research, 58, Jan. 1965, 233–6.

INBAR, MICHAEL: *The Differential Impact of a Game Simulating a Community Disaster.* American Behavioral Scientist, 10, Oct. 1966, 18–27.

MCQUIGG, R. BRUCE: *Micro Groups Studied Via Simulation.* Indiana University, Mimeo. (Undated).

REED, LUTON R.: *A Study of the Feasibility of Using Operational Simulation Techniques for Evaluating Administrative Skills Possessed by Instructional Communications Specialists.* Syracuse University, Doctoral Thesis, 1966.

SHEEHAN, T. JOSEPH: *Towards a System of Professional Education.* Irish Journal of Education, 1 (2), 1967, 141–9.

TWELKER, PAUL A.: *Classroom Simulation and Teacher Preparation.* School Review, 75, Summer 1967, 197–204.

CHAPTER FOUR

Academic gaming

There are certain simulations in which the elements of competition are an essential part of the structure. In these the participant plays either against other players or against the system. When this competitiveness is so clearly marked that an educational simulation depends upon it for its effectiveness then it is customary to call it an academic, business or management game. At the other end of the continuum of gaming there are the purely competitive games such as chess, card games, and the various games copyrighted and packaged by commercial firms and given to children at Christmas and on birthdays. It is not particularly profitable to draw a line between simulation and academic gaming, nor is it necessary to do so. A separate and different theory exists for the devising of games and for their use. People thrive on competition, and this temperament is suited by the competitive nature of gaming. It is a spirit that the schools have tried to develop and foster through the years by grading, examination marks and position in class statements on school reports. None the less, there is a considerable group of people for whom competition is anathema, and for them academic gaming may not be an effective way of learning.

There is another aspect of competition of which it is essential to be aware. This is the behaviour modifying effect. When people play games against each other they try to win. If this proves impossible using one pattern of behaviour then they modify their behaviour, and so learning takes place in the course of the game. The two behaviour patterns that emerge in gaming are playing to win, and when this is no longer possible, the person who cannot win tries to play in such a manner that he cannot lose. This is the technique of 'playing for a draw' which each of us must have experienced at the most trivial level when playing 'noughts and crosses'. It is also an accepted technique in sport at an international level, especially in cricket and soccer. Between the initial striving to win and the final compromise of playing for a draw we observe aspects of game-playing techniques like cheating and petulance manifest in such statements as 'I don't want to play any more'.

In any given situation it is as well to ask whether it is better to have competition or co-operation before deciding whether it is preferable to use a game or to use a simulation, for this is an essential difference between these two devices. There is a large body of educational opinion which nowadays says that the element of competition is not necessary in education, and research has been reported which indicates that learning takes place effectively in co-operative group situations. If this is so, and if the old rank and order concept in education is losing ground, we must be careful about the form of games played within the classroom. If the need to win does indeed modify participant behaviour, and if there is transfer of training from the game situation to the real life situation, then it could be the wrong kind of training that is transferred in a gaming exercise. For instance, in business or management games the desire not to lose may induce conservative behaviour and with it the unwillingness to take chances or calculated risks. Now, in the real life situation, the top executives may frequently need to take chances and to back their judgements. Such situations as diversification of interests, the introduction of new methods, the development of new markets, decisions to

51

export, and the employing of advisory staff are all risks. While rash decisions are not to be encouraged in any of these situations, a business based on ultra-conservative principles, which never makes decisions unless success has been pre-determined, must lose ground to the more adventuresome businesses which are in competition with it, and which are prepared to take risks.

On the other side of the ledger, the name itself is an aid in the classroom. A game suggests that it is not serious, that it is not work, that it is a break from the formality of the class-room. Use can be made of this, and against the background of fun, learning most certainly can take place. Games which are based on this assumption and which are now marketed will be discussed later in this chapter.

There are certain subjects or areas of study in the school curriculum, the sciences and mathematics for example, where the pupil can learn readily by doing. He can experiment and measure and can verify his hypotheses. Children who have become motivated in these subjects have their learning reinforced by participating. In the area of the social studies, learning by doing is not so easy. True, there are methods such as centres of interest, themes, projects, in which the child does participate. He cannot, however, make history, govern a country, represent its people, or plan its economy. The inability to participate has resulted in the social studies, and in fact the whole range of the humanities, taking on the mantle of an abstract and indeed a pointless exercise for many children, especially the less able. It might also be possible that the learning is not effective because it is abstract. A young child may not be moved by the great moments of history because he has not experienced them for himself.

This is to be regretted especially now, because we should be trying to foster in each child a tolerance and an understanding of both social and political issues that will enable him to make decisions based on reason rather than prejudice at both local and international levels. Games are being developed that enable him to experience, although vicariously, the making of history, or enable him to plan the economic growth of a

52

country, or to take part in policy decisions on an international level. In these games he can make mistakes and see that they are mistakes, act unwisely without fear of retribution, and reach reasoned decisions based on his own experiences. Abt Associates of Cambridge, Massachusetts, have devised a number of these games, and so has the team led by J. S. Coleman at Johns Hopkins University. In these games, the player assumes the role of a person in history, real or invented, and makes decisions that he might have taken. In this situation the player does not say . . . 'I might have done . . .', but as the office holder, or person, he says . . . 'I will do . . .', and sees the effects of his decisions. The greatest advantage of these games may be that they do in fact enable the participants to be actively engaged in the situation under discussion, but it is also possible that the effectiveness of such games springs from the fact that the participant learns without being aware that he is learning. In them his attitudes are being shaped under the pretext of play.

Much use is made of games in America for vocational training. There is a sense in which education at its terminal stage must concern itself with vocation no matter whether this terminal stage is at college level or in the final year of the secondary school. If this is so, then there is a use for games as vocational training devices. They can be used in the restrictive sense as career advising methods but they have a wider role to play than this. Vocational training is job training only in its narrowest definition. Before a person can live in our complex society he needs to know considerably more than the pre-requisites for and the prospects of a job. There is the whole area of social living to consider under the blanket definition of vocational training.

We live in a society which chooses to accept responsibility for the individual when he is ill, underprivileged, unemployed, too young or too old to support himself. The community has agreed to take care of each person, not only when he cannot take care of himself, but also under certain prescribed circumstances including illness, pregnancy, old age, and incapacity. Such care is not a privilege, although there is a persistent myth amongst the unthinking that it is. The nation is secretly ashamed of Social Security, and it wants beneficiaries to be thankful for the benefits received due to the benison of an undefined State. As a consequence we do not tell, or teach, young people their rights under our system; and cases of hardship continue through false pride and through the ignorance which we encourage in this area of joint responsibility while attempting to fight it in other places in education where we may meet it. Now simulation in general, and games in particular, can do a great deal to combat ignorance, to change opinion and prejudice, and to inform about these matters. If you tell a sixteen year old girl that she has certain rights as a mother, when she is pregnant she may not remember them. Besides, how few of us really know what these rights are? On the other hand, if it were possible to devise a game of some sort, possibly along the lines of MONOPOLY, in which these rights were illustrated, then the girl would know of them, and would be free to avail herself of the privileges that her condition entitled her to, should she ever need them. When the school leaving age is raised, and with the need to look beyond the four classroom walls for that prerequisite of education, *interest*, games as education for living have an established future. In practice, many people cannot devise games. Unlike simulations, they require special ability and specialized knowledge. Those people who have this flair will need to use it, as there will be an increasing demand for games that stress aspects of social living for school pupils of all ages.

It would be well at this stage to consider the theory of educational games. A confusion could exist between the kind of game a child finds in his Christmas stocking and educational games. The former have a prime fundamental need to entertain, while the fundamental need of educational games is to instruct. In them entertainment is an incidental or instrumental value, not the design objective. When an educational game is being devised, the first step is to ascertain the educational objectives of the game. Here it is necessary to decide on such items as the factual material that has to be included, the type of game that is required, whether card game, board game or paper and pencil game, the duration of each game, the number of players, and the constricts that will be placed on the playing of the game. For instance, at this time in the UK, classes have between thirty and forty pupils in them, there is limited space, and there are requirements about degree of noise and other disturbance factors during the playing of the games. If games can be devised which teach points clearly while at the same time fitting into the physical constraints of education they should prove popular. On the other hand, no matter how good they are as teaching devices, if the playing of them disturbs others, or if they induce in the participants behaviour that cannot be condoned in the social setting of the school, then they are no good to us as teaching aids.

When the general area, or time, or function of the game has been decided, what we might call a system analysis has been carried out. The next thing to be done is to analyse the form or sequence that the game will take. Here decisions about information, its methods of presentation, who shall possess it, how it will be passed on, will need to be made. It is at this stage that we must become sure about what the essential features are that we are trying to communicate. It is now that we must make a truly critical analysis of our teaching objectives, or of the key values in the situation in which the game is set. Thus, it might be felt at this stage in a business game that the essential feature of a business investment that might override all other considerations was *return on capital invested*. This would be considered an *absolute* value. Other values such as workers' security of job, public benefit, diversification of interest, cover of dividends and industrial relations would be seen as *instrumental* values. Similarly in the social sciences such absolute and instrumental values exist and must be recognized. Problems have to be recognized and techniques for the solving of these problems offered. When this has been done we will have identified the scope of what we are trying to achieve in the game, the main characters involved, the problems that these 'actors' have to face, alternative solutions to them or methods of dealing with the problems, and the probable consequences of these actions. Then we have designed a model.

The model may be analytical or it may be mathematically based, but it forms a constrict. It delineates the limits or bounds within which the exercise may take place. If the model is mathematical as it is in many business and computer-based games then the parameters can be represented by mathematical equations, and skill in the game is determined by the ability of the player to shape his behaviour so that it conforms more closely than that of other competitors to the pattern of these mathematical formulae. In either case, analytical or mathematical model, it now becomes necessary to translate the model into a form where it can be made available to the participant. The form must be such that it motivates the student as highly as possible.

It is difficult to obtain involvement by students unless elementary precautions are taken. The rules must be kept simple, and in these circumstances it is essential that a compromise between simplicity, which makes for ease of playing the game, and validity of the circumstances being portrayed is reached. Decisions also have to be made on the scope of the game. Is it better in a specific game to concentrate on a particular issue and avoid a wide cover of the subject, or is a comprehensive coverage of the topic required at the cost of detailed information and possibly credibility as well? Then it has to be decided how much drama must be introduced into the game with its accompanying emotive overtones and abandonment of calm reasoning and logic. In this area it seems axiomatic from past experience that if the emotional involvement is reduced then the motivation is reduced with it, but then cool analysis must be set against this motivation and emotional involvement. Of course, some of the decisions will be made or modified on the basis of classroom restrictions which include timetable, space limitations, and pupil behaviour patterns.

A game is tested by playing it. It is only then that the final snags can be seen. For instance, it is virtually impossible in the design stage to know how long it will take to play a game. If it is to be played in a classroom, it has to be geared to the normal fifty or so minutes period of the timetable. Suppose during a test play it is found to take much longer than this, then the design can be modified so that the game can be played in several parts, or broken up and made into several different games. Games such as WFF'N PROOF, ON SETS, EQUATIONS, designed by Layman E. Allen which are described later in the chapter have been divided as described above, so that WFF'N PROOF is now a system of twenty-one games most of which introduce new ideas or skills.

Two words that are in common usage in the American literature dealing with simulation and academic gaming are *scenario* and *profile*. In writing that has been done in this country these words have not been widely used. The scenario of a game means its background and setting while the profile means a case study related to the background of the game in some way. Frequently in 'home-made' games background information may be inadequate or possibly inaccurate. For instance, what is written may not agree with what is presented in another form; instructions may not be complete for all situations. Another common fault is lack of balance. It is always to be hoped that the game will involve all of the characters wholly and equally. Frequently this does not happen, as becomes obvious as soon as the game is first played. When inadequacies of this sort are brought to light decisions can be made either to re-write the part so that the character has more to do, or, if this proves too difficult, the character can be written out. If the case study or profile of a character is poorly done it is difficult for the participants to identify with him and this is an important point to remember and to look for in the preliminary game playing. It does not show up so clearly and participants in the preliminary exercise should be questioned on this point. And finally, pre-playing and testing allows an opportunity to add material to the game that will enhance its effectiveness or its appearance of reality.

Abt [1] has devised a typology of educational games and within it he has concluded that there are four fundamental game types. Games of *skill*, in which the outcome of the game depends on the ability of those playing the game. He classes business games in this category as well as golf and chess and indicates their virtue as being their rewarding of individual thought, skill and effort. They have the disadvantage of discouraging the less able and highlighting natural differences in ability.

Games of *chance* amongst which he includes dice, romance, roulette, and horse racing. In these the outcome is independent of player capabilities. These tend to encourage the slow learner because the winner is not selected on ability but at random and anyone can win. Abt does not hold games of pure chance in high regard in education for any other purpose than to illustrate probability theory. He feels that they tend to discount the value of planning and to obscure phenomenal relationships. On the other hand with repeated playing participants become more skilful in some games of 'chance'. Skill and chance are the two ends of one continuum of gaming with skill being at the stable or control end. The significant features of this continuum are that there is an element of competition essentially present, and that games are rule governed and played by individuals or teams against each other or against a system.

On another continuum under the general title of games, Abt has the terminal points of *reality* and *fantasy*. Amongst the former he includes simulations, drama and war games. He includes in the latter feelings of exhilaration such as are roused by music, dancing and skiing. Along this continuum the rules are designed to achieve a desired situation in which co-operation is usual, in which there is a dominant-dependent compensatory relationship within social groups. These groups observe the traditional and hierarchic relationships both within themselves and amongst others, and the technique most commonly used is that of role-play and total involvement and committal as opposed to the abstraction and specialization of the skill-chance continuum previously described. It will be obvious that the second of these continua is not really gaming at all, at least not as it has been defined and described in this book. Although the first continuum describes gaming the second is descriptive of simulation and is as good a way of distinguishing between them as any other. Abt (p. 14) states . . . 'The stable poles of games activities tend to be skill and fantasy. Chance degrades into fantasy, reality when understood becomes differentiated into games of skill.'

There will always be those amongst us who oppose change in anything, and education has many amongst its numbers who will not change either their methods or their beliefs. For them games will be anathema because their ideas are such that they see little that is educational in anything that is pleasurable. But educational games and indeed simulations are serious and significant; they completely involve the student, changing his attitude to learning from passive to eager activity. It is not necessary to compare games with traditional classroom methods; it is certain that if the game is well constructed it must be at least as good a teaching method as chalk and talk, or projects, given all the other variables inseparable from any class-room situation.

Pupils certainly are often much more highly motivated by games than by other methods of conveying information. They learn skills of the problem-solving kind, of communication, and of co-operation readily through the use of games. Younger children learn from games to develop concepts through observing interrelations within the context of what they are doing, and success in games of skill brings immediate reinforcement of their behaviour. There is a vast amount that young children have not experienced at first hand and for this reason verbal instruction is not a very satisfactory method for inculcating abstract concepts. When dealing with abstraction it is necessary to move from the specific to the general. The specific implies experience in a particular situation, and the game situation can give this to the young child. From games he can come to understand concepts such as feasibility, probability and impossibility within the gaming context and can be encouraged to extend these conceptions beyond games into direct experiences in other areas.

The older child who is not academically gifted wants to see the point of what he is learning. If he is to be enthusiastic about it, it must have an immediate relevance. While the able child may be content to learn because the material forms a

59

groundwork for what is to come, the less able need to be assured that what they are learning will be of use to them, if not today, then tomorrow at the latest. They tend to see learning in value terms relative to the job of the future or relative to qualification for this job. Amongst the older children in secondary schools the humanities are not generally popular subjects although there are many teachers who teach them well. Now presumably children learn about the humanities because they are the basis of civilized communal living and the cornerstone of our society. It is possible that they deserve a more prominent place and a far greater emphasis in the schools' curricula than they now enjoy. Their message is, nonetheless, hard to convey to reluctant children and so an effort must be made to disguise the instruction in a form that is pleasant. Such a form is gaming and it is in this part of the curriculum that games will have their first and most important application in the next few years. Their great virtue is the high degree of motivation they build up in the children, and they break down some of the inborn restrictions due to the existence of the nineteenth century hangover of classrooms as separate boxes to parcel and divide children into neat groups administratively easy to handle.

While gaming is being practised and games are being devised by teachers to fit their own classroom conditions, there is little communication between interested parties in this country either in gaming or simulation. This is a very different situation from that which applies currently in the United States of America. There are many teams concerned with gaming in America but only three of the best known will be mentioned in this chapter together with examples of their games. Abt Associates is a firm in business to make games to clients' wishes. If a firm or an education authority wishes to have a game developed to teach a specific thing Abt Associates will co-operate with them and devise a game which becomes the client's property after it has been constructed and tested. They have worked for a large number of clients in a wide range of activities, and some of their games have enjoyed a great deal of publicity. Abt [2] has compared educational games with programmed instruction, case studies and T-Groups, and has found gaming has advantages over all these other methods so far as motivation is concerned. He also indicates that it is as effective in teaching as any of the other methods, that it has fewer limitations, and that its scope is at least as wide as any other method. Abt also points out that games shorten the training process, and so are 'less expensive' than conventional training methods. He offers no facts or figures to substantiate this claim, however, and it would seem to be a difficult claim to substantiate. Nor is it necessary to justify the use of games on this basis at least as far as education is concerned. If something of value is to be taught, if some significant or essential point is to be made, then the transmission is the significant thing. If this can be done effectively and efficiently by conventional methods then these methods can be used without need to have recourse to games. But if there are numbers of students who are reluctant to learn by one method, or who cannot grasp an idea when it is presented in one way, do not good teachers cast about for alternative ways of presentation? Gaming is justified on this basis alone, and until we have cost-efficiency studies in education, it is a pointless exercise to rest the claim of a technique on its cost. Most of us in education do not even know the relative costs of the different ways of duplicating materials so we are unlikely to know the cost of teaching, or learning, irrespective of the method of presenting the learning.

On the other hand, flexibility is a good point. If there is to hand a teaching method that works for the above average, the average, and the below average pupil at the same time, and if it teaches them the things that it is desired to learn, then it is a good method. Games would seem to do this, judging by a mass of literature which claims this as the case. Whether it does so for *all* students is unlikely, but that it does so for most students is probable.

Abt Associates have developed many educational and business games. Several of these are intended for use in primary schools, including the infant classes. There is a reading readiness series for the kindergarten and first year infant classes, and various games for other age ranges in the primary range. Included is a series of three games designed for use with eleven-year-old children as part of a curriculum course on 'Man'. They are played on boards and are named Seal Hunting, Caribou Hunting, and Bushman Exploring and Gathering. The last is a two-phase game.

The game of MARKET was developed for the Elementary Games Project, Industrial Relations Center, University of Chicago, and is designed to show to 6th grade (12-year-old) American students how prices are fixed or determined in a market economy. The game is played by teams of two persons representing wholesalers, retailers and customers respectively. Each team of customers has a shopping board divided into thirty squares in four different colours, and the team has to cover the board with goods represented by tokens of the same colour as the square on which they are placed in order to win the game. Red tokens represent essential goods which the consumer has to purchase, blue and yellow tokens represent complementary goods which have little value unless they are paired. The green squares can be filled with any goods the purchasing team wants. They try to buy goods at the cheapest possible price. At the start of the game the retailers and the wholesalers receive tokens representing goods, and have inventories on which they must keep track of all of the goods sold. The wholesalers tend to specialize but the retailers have a wide range of goods. The pattern of distribution is not known by the whole group of players.

The game is in two parts, the first part being tactical with teams deciding on the prices they would like to pay for the goods on offer, or the price they think the goods will sell for. There is a place on the inventory sheets for these prices to be recorded, and during the second, bargaining phase when goods are actually sold and bought, these prices also have to be recorded. These separate columns are then used as the basis for post-game discussion. From the differences in these recorded prices, and armed with knowledge of goods in demand and goods not sought after, the laws of supply and demand can be developed by the student. There is movement in this game with purchasers visiting the stores and storekeepers visiting the wholesalers, but the game is quickly over. It is scheduled to occupy only about twenty minutes of class time, allowing plenty of time for the post-game stage of discussion and rule establishment.

One outstanding feature of the American game is the frenetic preoccupation with time. In the authors' experience of various games this is the one feature that they seem to have in common, that the phase must be completed in a certain number of minutes. One game even supplies an egg timer so that there shall be no doubt about the sands running out! Again in our experience this does not suit the average British schoolchild, nor can we see much point in it.

The Association of American Geographers has developed a series of simulation-games for the teaching of geography at high school level. Called the High School Geography Project, and based on the University of Colorado at Boulder, it has made an honest attempt to teach geography by new methods. Amongst the units that incorporate something of gaming or simulating are the following: The Growth of Cities, The Geography of Culture Change, Manufacturing, Agriculture, and Political Processes. One unit of these was designed by Abt Associates. This game, SECTION, attempts to show students a conflict of interests amongst citizens of a fictitious state; it illustrates the use of strategies, and shows the relation of political decisions to resources, public investment and developments. A demonstration kit containing sample activities from several different units is available for one dollar. Sets of the printed materials for the unit 'The Growth of Cities', cost four dollars and those of the Geography of Culture Change cost 2.50 dollars. No audiovisual aids are included at this price. The address is: The High School Geography Project, P.O. Box 1095, Boulder, Colorado 80302 and a newsletter which is published periodically can be obtained from this address free on request.

The second group of people concerned with the gaming aspects of simulation in America is that from the Department of Social Relations, Johns Hopkins University, led by

Professor James S. Coleman. They have come to the conclusion that the structure of the instruction in a school is as important as the content of the lessons. They also feel that the methods of instruction used in American schools (and which are also used in our own schools) no longer suit the needs of the school population. These methods were introduced at a time when fewer children stayed on at school than do now. The children who did remain were the children of professional parents, were highly motivated, and for them the preoccupation of school with content and formal methods fitted well with their expectations. The Johns Hopkins group also point out that when these methods were first introduced our relationship with children was very different from that which applies at present. In those days we exerted an authority over them because adults occupied traditional authority positions. The father, the teacher, the vicar – all could expect to be respected because they were these things. In those days of strict upbringing there was little thought of persuading the child, the norm being to order. The reward for such children was the approval of adult society.

As we are well aware, there are many children for whom the approval of adult society is no inducement today. For some indeed such approval may well be anathema. In the terminal stages of education there is little motivation in the classroom, and we have come to recognize this, and have taken such steps to overcome it as establishing curriculum development centres so that the schools can be prepared for the raising of the school leaving age. Even where we deal with above average children from middle and upper class backgrounds who are highly motivated and who expect to advance their education to university or college level, we find that they do not seek our approval so much as they turn to their own peers for their rewards.

Boocock and Coleman [3] find three major defects in American secondary education. These are that it is designed to teach for a long range future, that the curriculum is enforced and little of it is of a voluntary nature, and that the teacher has a dual role as teacher and judge in which he not only teaches but awards grades which can have a large determining effect on his pupil's future. It is true that these strictures apply here also, although few teachers would find much of significance in the third one. The number of times that a teacher has experienced lasting resentment from a pupil because only five marks were awarded instead of the seven the pupil felt entitled to must be very few in any teacher's lifetime. It would also seem to be false logic to say on the one hand that the pupil would rather have the approval of his peers than of the adults in his role set, and then to say that he resents the teacher in his role as judge. One might well feel that the pupil does not everlastingly care about his grade in the majority of cases.

Coleman and his associates think that simulation games go a long way towards overcoming these defects in American education. To their minds these games which are based on social, cultural and economic models have marked advantages to offer. They feel that they bring the future into the child's present by allowing him to play roles that he will have to play *or to be aware of* as an adult in the community. Then there is an immediate reason for playing a game: in a game the player plays to win and success is an immediately reinforcing result. If a player does not win, it is hoped that he will learn by playing the game the necessary techniques for winning. The player plays those roles he knows he will play as an adult and can see that he must learn during the course of the games both the special skills and the moral attitudes necessary for them.

Like most people who have had anything to do with simulation, the Johns Hopkins workers stress the motivating aspect of games and of simulation generally. As a result of this motivation discipline ceases to be a problem because it comes from the child himself. In the authors' experience, this is a very true and telling point indeed. Finally Boocock and Coleman point out that games are self-judging, with the winner being clearly decided by the outcome, and so they release the teacher from his dual role.

The first three games designed by the group were intended to

65

instruct or to shape attitudes in separate areas. The first was a career game in which teams of between two and four players competed against each other. A cleverly designed game, it made the students think of their future careers in terms of qualifications and of investment of time, money and effort. An element of chance and random selection introduced into the game by means of spinners and dice gave it a certain unpredictability which added spice to it. Such a game has a wide application in this country and would make a pleasant change from the perpetual pamphlet with which some career teachers still paper their walls to justify their allowances. The Johns Hopkins game would require modification but possibly a teacher might be able to design one of his own which would then be useful to other teachers in other schools.

There is a need to show children not only that they have a democratic representation of the people, but also that the system works reasonably well. To do this teachers are even prepared to drag out of their dank hiding places such things as lobbying and 'dealing' and to show how these tactics oil the wheels of democracy. In the second of the Johns Hopkins games these principles are brought to light. The game is designed to be played by a group of from six to ten players each of whom represents a legislator who is making decisions on a public issue. Cards are dealt which tell him his constituents' attitudes to various issues and he votes accordingly. For instance a card might say the equivalent of . . . 'government's medical care of the old . . . 20 per cent for, 80 against'. If the Medicare bill got through the legislature then the possessor of this card would lose $80 - 20 = 60$ points. In order to get this bill rejected, the holder of the card may, in the game, make deals with holders of other cards offering his backing for or against issues on which they have strong feelings. He may later refuse this support if his bill is voted on early in the agenda. Lying and cheating are possible and may pay dividends, but this presumably does no more than reflect the actual working of government. The point of the game is to show what really happens, rather than to teach some vague idealization seldom if ever achieved in practice. At the con-

66

clusion of the game each legislator's points are totalled to
determine who is re-elected. Like WFF'N PROOF the game
can be played at several levels of complexity. Another game
is that of a simulated community disaster, with players acting
out roles. It is claimed in favour of these games that specific
information can be learned from them and that a perspective,
an awareness, is created so that the players see the complexity
of future social situations about which they had thought little
previously.

The games discussed so far have all had social bases of some
kind. The third group of workers has devised a series of games
based on mathematical models. The earliest of these games
were constructed by Layman E. Allen, then a professor of
Law at Yale University and now at the University of Michigan.
This fact of his professing law is presumably responsible for
the one outstandingly bad thing about these games: it takes
another lawyer to understand the rules. The games are
ingenious and at least one of them will be described in the
chapter on general classroom applications. They differ from
the other kinds of game because they do not try to shape
attitudes but have a preoccupation with content. This preoccupation is well disguised and is contained in a framework in
which it is fun to play the game once the rules have been
learned. The games can be played merely for pleasure, but
especially in ON SETS and EQUATIONS players learn in
spite of themselves.

BIBLIOGRAPHY

1. ABT, C. C.: *Education is Child's Play*. Paper read at the Lake Arrow-
   head Conference on Innovation in Education, Dec. 1965.
2. ABT, C. C.: *Twentieth Century Teaching Techniques*. Reprinted from
   The Faculty, 30, August 1966, American Institute of Banking
3. BOOCOCK, S. S. *and* COLEMAN, J. S.: *Games with Simulated
   Environments in Learning*. Sociology of Education, 39, Summer 1966,
   215–36.

Simulation and gaming in education
RELATED READING

NESBITT, W. A.: *Simulation Games for the Social Studies Classroom.* Vol. 1, No. 1, New Dimensions Series, Foreign Policies Association, New York. Undated.

SHUBIK, MARTIN (Ed.): *Game Theory and Related Approaches to Social Behavior.* John Wiley, New York, 1964.

CHAPTER FIVE

Games in the classroom

When traditional teaching methods are used in the classroom there is an automatically induced dichotomy between the teacher and the taught because these methods are based upon, and depend upon, the traditional authority patterns. Thus the teacher, the vicar, the policeman, have in the past warranted respect by virtue of the positions that they occupy and this respect does not have to be secured by achievement. The holders of such positions hold what sociologists call an 'ascribed' status. In education today this is largely enjoyed only at the highest levels of training, notably in the universities. It is still in existence in these places, not because the education is necessarily enjoyed for itself, but because of the expectancy that the final award has merit in the eyes of future employers. The possession of this final award, a degree, shows the prospective employer that its possessor is a person who has conformed within the traditional pattern and has reached a certain prescribed standard of academic attainment.

Even in the universities the traditional authority pattern could not succeed were it not for the artificially induced situation that there are more contenders for places than there are places to offer them. And recently, despite these constraints, we see a growing unrest amongst these students in the final stages of education. They doubt the value of selection methods, of content and of teaching techniques. It has long been offered as argument that if a patient goes to see his doctor, or a client visits his lawyer, he does so for advice and because he is not in a position to decide what he wants for himself. So also, says the traditionalist in education, the student does not know what he wants and so he must accept what we give him though it does not seem to have any immediate relevance.

But lawyers lose cases that they might have won, and doctors make mistakes, and their clients know that they have done so. In the same way teachers in the past have used methods that could have been improved upon and their clients – the pupils – have known. Boredom, inattention, and misbehaviour have told the teacher that the pupils were aware of these faults. The alert teacher can use such symptoms as an early warning system and search for new methods of presentation of lesson content. This search is not for the 'best' method, but for the best method in this instance and with this particular pupil or group. Some such teachers have devised games and used them in their classrooms.

There are three fundamental processes that are present in any successful lesson. They must all be present in an ordered pattern. For convenience let us call these processes *control*, *interest* and *content*, although there are many other names by which they might be called. Control is the first and most important ingredient of any lesson. It may be obtained in many different ways, some better than others, some based on mutual respect and others based on the rigidity of the traditional authority pattern. Most of us are familiar with the teacher whose voice is always raised in frenetic wrath, and who is often inarticulate with anger. His control is based on fear, and his preoccupation is with content. For him the child is a sausage skin to be stuffed with the gristle and fat of knowledge before it is wrapped and tied and passed on to the next stage of processing. For him the acme of success is the number of passes in external examinations his pupils achieve, for this is his way of showing his ability to the world outside, and his way

70

of extracting praise and approval from that world. At the other end of the continuum is the gentle control exercised by good teachers in infant schools where today's revolution in teaching methods is most clearly to be seen. Control is necessary but the method of obtaining it is of basic importance. Before a child can be taught he must be prepared to listen and to participate, and hence the prime importance of control.

Having got the pupil prepared to learn, the next thing is to make him want to learn. This is the reason why interest is of such importance. There is a whole world engaged in presenting goods in such a way that people want to use them. The goods that are sold via advertising agencies are probably no better than other goods that are not advertised, but they *seem* to be better and that is more than half the battle. Advertising makes things seem good, fresh or exciting, and makes them desirable. We do not do enough 'advertising' in education, and yet what education has to offer is more important than margarine with ten per cent of real butter in it, and more significant than the rough hands which are an inevitable consequence of washing up with brand X. But we are changing in education, and this change is a convection which has risen through the infant schools to the junior schools and has now reached the secondary modern schools. New methods are in use, and the classroom is no longer the prison that it was in the past. With luck the new ideas may soon permeate the centres of higher education where the third of our elements is held to be of prime importance. Content certainly is important, but it is arguable that there is an essential body of knowledge which must be passed on to our pupils in the austere setting of the classroom, and which cannot be passed on anywhere else. Does a child become a better adult for the knowing of Euclidean geometry, simultaneous equations, Latin declensions or any other of the standard pieces of information that we currently have handed on to our pupils out of a respect for the vanished past?

But what has this to do with games? Nothing directly except to indicate what many already know, that there is a case to be made for change, and a need to look at what we are

71

doing and see if there are other more vital and more motivating ways of accomplishing our ends.

If we have a classroom situation in which the 'them and us' relationship prevails it is likely that control will be in the form of a constraint and interest will not be spontaneous. If the teacher is a director of operations who plans all the moves, he has to make sure that he makes no mistakes. Are such people not using authoritarian methods to teach democratic principles? The methods may well be all right for the conforming children of middle class homes which accept the values of the schools automatically, but are they suitable for those children who come from homes that are out of step with the school? From homes whose values are totally at variance with those of the school? And there are a lot of these children: they leave school as soon after their fifteenth birthday as they can. The State, recognizing this, is to apply the force of the law to make them spend another year at school. Unless ways can be found of making them interested in what they are doing, then teaching will be at best an unpleasant and unrewarding experience.

Simulations and classroom games could supply part of the answer to some of the problems that have been mentioned above. A game permits the pupil a large amount of freedom of action, and the teacher does not have to become involved nor need he dominate proceedings as much as he usually does in orthodox teaching methods. However, there is a great deal more involvement on the part of the pupils when simulations or games are played. Because games impose certain rules, and because pupils are involved, problems of control and interest are virtually solved. Discipline is self-imposed and the teacher becomes a guide and not a director. There is motivation in games: that is one absolutely certain thing about them, and as a result the element of competition essentially present in games is significant. In behaviourist terms, reinforcement is, if not immediate, at least fairly rapid. It is specific and is given by winning the game. It is not so abstract a thing as a tick or a grade. There is also a spirit of co-operation present in games, many of which are played by groups of players in

72

competition with other similar groups. The competition is between peers and is not sterile as it might be if a student competes with a text book.

Games, of course, suggest that the content is not serious and that there is no emphasis on factual knowledge, but in fact one of the *easiest* things about games is the incorporation of factual knowledge. The essential difference between this form of presentation and that of the more traditional methods is that the factual knowledge built into a game is needed immediately, and so is easily remembered, whereas the factual knowledge of a prescribed curriculum has to be stored against the *possibility* of its being used some time in the future. It may be that this use will only be the passing of examinations, and so students have developed a facility for remembering, only to forget as soon as the need to remember has passed. How many of us at some stage learned the answer to some question we thought was an examination certainty, and how few of us still retain that knowledge. If we decide to construct a game that will teach fact, obviously we will have to include factual information in the game. Because the facts are part of the rules or conditions of the game they will become known and remembered. Thus as a way of conveying fact, games have certain advantages.

It is possible that not enough has been said about commitment and motivation. When, in education, we cannot explain or justify what we are attempting to do, we use emotion charged words like belief or faith. Religious education as it was practised in the past was a classic example of this: no effort of explanation was made in religious instruction lessons, but, of course, the subject frequently was not taught at all. What was substituted was Biblical history and historical geography. Alternatively, the child was told to 'sit still and listen and one day you may understand'. At a Christmas service in a primary school known to the authors, the local vicar, the chairman of the managers, and various other local dignitaries each read one of the nine lessons. The vicar read the one about the immaculate conception. A parent, seeking to find out what this all meant to her nine year old daughter asked her on the way

F

home what a virgin was and what conception was. 'I don't know,' she replied. 'Mummy, what's for tea?'

It has been recognized by many of those who teach religious education, that moral decisions are the ones of most significance, and that indoctrination is a poor basis for reaching rational and mature decisions. Here then is a field in which simulation and academic gaming could play an important part because it does commit the participant, and there is no other technique in existence in teaching which motivates and involves the learner more. This area of study has not been explored by the designers of academic games up till the present, as far as can be determined by the authors, but more will be said about applications of simulation in the field of moral education in a later chapter.

Games do present problems for the class teacher, but in general the problems are already there, and it might be better to say that some difficulties are highlighted. It is certainly true that there is a percentage of people who do not like the idea of direct competition with their peers. Just how high this percentage is is not known, but it is possible that it is a significant one. Students who fall in this category are loath to participate in academic games, and tend to sit and do nothing, or as little as is possible. For this reason games have been criticized, but do all students participate fully in any other kind of activity or teaching method? We are well aware that a large percentage of children has no heart for organized games of the soccer, rugby, hockey, tennis, cricket variety, but we persist with them.

Two things make us more aware of the non-participant in an academic game than in a traditional lesson. The first is that the teacher has a less precise and exacting role. He is not required to be in front of the class directing and ordering, and so has leisure time in which to observe. The same non-participant in academic games may well be hiding his indifference behind a book in a formal lesson. The second thing that sharpens our awareness is that the great majority of pupils are keen participants and their keenness and involvement tends to highlight the indifference of the few who do not want to play.

Another problem that arises but which is easily overcome is an organizational one. Especially if a teacher uses a home-made game there are certain to be difficulties such as faulty instructions, directions that are too complex, and the major problem of time. Educational games have to be built into an existing set of constricts, they have to fit into classrooms and into periods of lesson time. These are difficult things to do and frequently games have to be modified after their initial design. There is a need for careful and detailed planning before a game is as effective as it can be. On the other hand, the process is relatively inexpensive, involves most of the children deeply, allows them freedom from the usual teacher-dominated class-room situation, allows them to make decisions and allows the acquisition of knowledge in an enjoyable manner.

One of the reasons that gaming is not more popular is that there are relatively few games available. Nearly all the games that will be described later in this chapter are games designed for the American situation, and are of limited use here in their present form except to give an indication of the kind of work that has been going on in the United States. This is not true of the mathematical games where a knowledge of content is the important factor, but it is true of those games where attitudes are to be shaped.

Again, one cannot be sure how effective is learning by games because it is hard to measure accurately. Like other educational innovations, academic gaming has its band of enthusiasts, and like other educational innovations its effectiveness may well be reduced when it is operated by those who are not themselves committed. It is certainly true that games are more positively structured than some other innovations have been, and their effectiveness depends far less on teacher enthusiasm than some other recently introduced educational advancements. Whether games teach facts better than other methods, whether they do teach values or encourage children to think more critically are not easy questions to answer. They may not even be relevant questions to ask because it might be thought that games justify themselves merely by being alternative methods to those currently employed, and which are highly

75

effective in the case of certain individuals who have not previously been motivated. There is also a tendency to be avoided in the assessing of the worth of games – the tendency to generalize from the particular, the tendency to judge all games from the one we happen to know and to base our opinions of games on that. There are, without doubt, good games and bad, games that teach and games which do not, and circumstances under which any given game can be either most effective or absolutely useless. It is also certain that the effectiveness of a game depends to a large extent on the quality of the teacher. The teacher has a different role in academic gaming, but it is nevertheless an equally important, although less dominating one than that of the traditional teacher.

We can define games as simulations with a competitive element in them. This is a fairly artificial division, but a large part of the work done in the field of classroom simulation and gaming has depended on this competitive element, possibly because teachers like to be able to measure the achievements of their pupils and have grown accustomed to doing so in the past. In the following part of this chapter a number of games will be described and an effort will be made to indicate where these games can be obtained. From this descriptive work it is to be hoped that teachers who are keen to try out the method will be able to see the areas in which academic games have been used in the past. This part may also give some teachers the incentive to design games of their own.

DESCRIPTIONS OF GAMES

1. MATHEMATICAL GAMES

One of the leading workers in the field of mathematical games is Layman E. Allen of the University of Michigan. He has designed a number of games which are played with dice and are primarily intended to teach specific content rather than to shape ideas or to inculcate values. They can be played purely for enjoyment with no emphasis being placed on the underlying content, but once the rules have been understood, the ability to use the content is axiomatic. The most famous of these games, which will be described herein, is WFF'N PROOF which stands for *well formed formula and proof*. It was designed by Allen while he was a member of the faculty of the Yale University Law School, and it was probably his desire to identify the game with the place that was responsible for the name.* Like other games in the series it suffers from the serious defect that the rules are so complexly worded that it is difficult to play for some time. Of course, this need not be a problem for children because it is to be expected that the teacher would first learn how to play and then tell the children in easy stages.

The basis of the game is propositional logic and the notation of the Polish mathematician Jan Lukasiewicz is used. The kit consists of a book of instructions, playing mats, a timer, and 36 logic blocks or dice attractively mounted in a binder. Eighteen of the dice have capital letters on their faces, and the other eighteen have lower case letters. Of the six capital letters, five are significant, namely

N which means it is false that . . .

C which suggests implication, i.e. if x then y.

A which suggests disjunction, i.e. either x or y or both.

K which suggests conjunction, i.e. both x and y.

E which suggests condition, i.e. x if and only if y.

The lower case letters p, q, r, s, are proposition variables.

There are a total of thirteen ideas introduced and used repeatedly in the playing of the game of WFF'N PROOF. These are the definition of a WFF, the definition of a PROOF and eleven rules of inference. In the series there are twenty-one games and the thirteen ideas are presented very gradually. A player proceeds to the next game only after he has had considerable practice in using the idea introduced in the last one and has had the chance to see at least some of the relationships between ideas learned up to that time.

A WFF is defined as a given expression which fulfils one of the following conditions:

1. it is a 'p', 'q', 'r', or 's'.

* The Wff'n Proof song – 'We're two little sheep who have lost our way, "Ba, ba, ba",' etc.

2. it is the expression formed when an '*N*' is immediately followed by a WFF.
3. it is the expression formed when '*C*', '*A*', '*K*' or '*E*', is followed immediately by two WFFs.

A rule of inference is a method of deriving new WFFs from WFFs you already have. In the first game, the players each have three dice, two with small letters and the third with capital letters on its faces. These are the 'shaking set', and after they have been rolled the player has to make the longest WFF that it is possible to make from the letters face uppermost on the cubes. If he succeeds in doing so, he is given – from his 'stockpile' – another cube with capital letters, and as long as he continues to be successful he continues to get additional cubes in such a way that he has either one more cube with lower than with upper case letters, or equal numbers of each. If, at any roll, another player can make a longer WFF than the person who rolled the dice, then the roller has to put one of his dice back into his stockpile. The winner is the person who uses up his stockpile of ten dice first. This first game is intended to show the new player the rules for making WFFs and to let him understand the concept of a WFF.

The rules of inference come one at a time from the third game onwards and from this point the object of each game is to construct a proof using only those rules of inference that have been introduced up to that stage. This may appear to be obvious, but it could well be that an experienced player who had played through the series of twenty-one games could be at an advantage with an inexperienced player unless this rule applied.

The games are a formal logic system in their own right and do not depend on any premise or supposition outside the game system. On the other hand, the rules are formal and stylized, and although long, wordy and involved, can be learned with patience and help. The games can then be played as chess or draughts might be played just for fun with no expectation of learning from them. If, at a later time, the logic system was required, it would already be known to the participant who was familiar with the rules. Allen [1] has described WFF'N PROOF as an 'autotelic' or self motivating activity, and it also has elements of the 'Skinnerian' stimulus-response type of programme.

Another of Allen's games that seems to have more general use in the classroom especially amongst mixed ability groups of different ages is the game of EQUATIONS. It is a fascinating game whose rules, although formidable, are nowhere near as complex as are those of WFF'N PROOF. The game is cleverly designed and a teacher could design a large part of a mathematics scheme around this game alone. If there is a British retailer for these games the authors are unaware of him; there is certainly a need for a source of supply and the need will increase.

The significance of this aside is that this spirit of competition has permeated the WFF'N PROOF series of games. At the Nova High Schools complex at Fort Lauderdale where these and other games are played in a system directed by Robert Allen, there is an academic 'Olympiad' in which teams from various parts of the country compete. It is felt that the lad who can play WFF'N PROOF well has the right to feel the same sense of achievement that his more muscular brother in the athletics squad feels. It is reasonably certain that even the Greeks did not have a word for that.

Other games that are similar in format and which are valuable in the classroom are THE REAL NUMBERS GAME and ON SETS, the latter of which is useful for explaining set theory. The games are useful, cheap, and are enjoyable to play once the complexity of the rules have been mastered. It would seem that their greatest advantage in this country might be to motivate the slow learner, and as an occupation for the pupil who has finished his work and has time to fill, rather as chess might be used. They are possibly as intellectually stimulating as chess, and one can arrange classes rather like whist drives or tennis ladders so that good players play against other good players and weaker ones against others of similar ability, thus ensuring that few people are discouraged by being beaten too frequently.

2. GAMES FOR THE SOCIAL SCIENCES

a International

In this area of academic gaming the distinction between simulation and gaming is not well defined. The games that are described here do, however, all have that element of direct competition in which person competes against person or group competes directly with group. The competition is a key feature of each.

DANGEROUS PARALLEL is a game devised by the Foreign Policy Association of 345 East 46th Street, New York, N.Y. 10017. It is not commercially available, being still in the developmental stage. While it is not the aim of the game to recapitulate history, it is based on the Korean crisis and the crossing of the 38th parallel. Imaginary names have been given to countries and a map is supplied showing an imaginary part of the world. In the game students in the age range 16 to 18 play the parts of decision-making members of cabinets faced with an international situation. The game is played by twenty-four or more players divided into six teams each of which represents a nation. Some of the nations are great powers and some are small nations. In each team there is a chief minister and the other members of his team take on the roles of other cabinet ministers such as foreign affairs and defence. The serious international crisis that has developed at the start of the game is caused by the attack of one small nation on another. One of the great powers has already become involved in the conflict and two others are in danger of involvement; there is a consequent threat of nuclear war.

The game is a 'programmed' one with a series of moves. For each move there is a series of twenty-four alternatives, four each for the six nations. Moves involve policy planning, negotiations, diplomacy, and decision making. All nations make their decisions simultaneously on a signal from the teacher, and the teacher is able to announce the consequences of the actions immediately. It is hoped that the game will enable students to obtain an analytical approach to international affairs and that this approach will have a carryover to adult life. Learning by doing is also an important aspect of this, and indeed all games. In this particular one, the players learn something of how nations behave by having to make decisions rather than by just talking. They also experience the feeling of what it is like to be a part of a culture that is not American; for instance, to be a member of a weak and powerless nation. The game is, in the opinion of its designers, a valuable tool to set the stage for subsequent teaching. With this modest claim there would be few who would cavil.

Here is a starting point for the class teacher who wants to design his own game: all the necessary ingredients for a successful game are contained in the information above. First select an incident in history from which a crisis situation developed. There are many of these as each of us knows only too well . . . the American Civil War with its commercial, cotton and land use background, the Cuban crisis, the October Revolution, the rise of Nazism, the start of the First and Second World Wars, the Vietnam conflict, and so forth.

Now gather the background information such as groups involved, incidents that were prime contributing causes and other relevant matter. At this stage there is a need to be discriminating and to make sure that undue influence is not given to detail that is relatively unimportant. After the grouping has been decided on, it is important to decide on the composition of the groups and the duties and responsibilities of the members of each group. The hardest part of the task is finished at this point and subsequent decisions determine the form of the game, the incidents that will be used, and the length of playing time for each stage of the game. Finally the game is shaped by repeated trial and error. These repeated trials will show up weaknesses that you as the designer will not be able to see in any other way.

There are various pitfalls against which it pays to be on guard. Questions you must ask are . . . 'Are all the players occupied during the game?' If one is not and he becomes bored or not involved he can easily spoil the game. 'Are there any inaccuracies or contradictions or false information in the background information?', 'Have I got the running time approximately right?', 'Will the game fit into the physical space available in the classroom?'. These last two are the major constraints imposed by the teaching situation. When you are satisfied on all of these counts, finally ask yourself whether it does in fact seem that the game is actually doing what you had expected it to do. Of course, we can never be sure that we are doing exactly what we hope, however we teach, because our powers to communicate are not highly enough developed, but careful questioning will get a response which may reassure you or alternatively make you want to recast the design of the game. It is wise not to assume that enjoyment on the part of the players affirms that appropriate learning has taken place. Pleasure in playing the game may be a *necessary* condition for learning but it is certainly not a *sufficient* one. We hope, that as a result of the game, an attitude may have been changed, that a point of view may have become less prejudiced or that some facts or processes may have been learned. Skilful discussion and questioning will give a good indication of whether these goals have been met.

Bloomfield and Padelford [2] have this to say in justification of political gaming:

> . . . In a role-playing game the interaction generates a self-sustaining reaction that develops its own momentum and course independent of the limits or boundaries with which the analyst starts out. Inherent in this process is the potent challenge of unpredictability and the equally potent value of exposure to the antagonistic will of another who proceeds from entirely different assumptions. Neither of these factors can be derived from solitary meditation or co-operative discussion. In this sense an affirmative answer is possible to the general question, 'Is political gaming useful?'; and this conclusion emerges as the clearest finding from our experimentation.

The Foreign Policy Association has extended its international simulation by using the medium of television to involve larger numbers of students. For this they have selected the 1950 crisis in which Tito's Yugoslavia rejected Soviet domination. Three 'nations' are involved and situations are put out on television unrehearsed. Participating schools are in touch with the TV station by phone, ringing in their decisions and observing the effects of them on the screen. At the conclusion of the programme, each class is asked to view the changed international situation and write a letter of advice on policy to the chief minister at the TV station.

Other games, involving international situations have been described by Cherryholmes [4] and Gearon [6]. Kaplan and Gordon [7] criticize Gearon's 'War and Peace' game and point out a number of defects, namely that while the game is enjoyable, it presents over-simplified and misleading facts and processes to the players. For example, war costs nothing to the victor; all players have complete information. It would seem to be the basis of their argument that a game must present complex processes in a meaningful way, and involve the students in the operation of such processes.

The Western Behavioral Sciences Institute has a game called CRISIS which costs 35 dollars for a 25 student kit, but a sample kit can be obtained for one dollar. This game does not use a real situation – the action involves six fictitious nations involved in an imaginary situation concerned with the mining of a mineral of strategic importance. Decisions are written and the effects of these decisions are communicated to the players at regular intervals. This is a fairly fluid game situation and alliances, summit conferences, police forces on an international scale, can all be arranged according to the players' wishes. It is alleged to be effective with pupils from the age of twelve and on up to post graduate level.

b Social Games

i *Vocational Training.* The LIFE CAREER game was devised by Sarane Boocock of Johns Hopkins University in order to help young people with their choice of vocations. The game is designed to teach about decisions that people in our society have to make at various times in their lives; the interrelationship between education and job prospects; factors which affect a person's success in his job, marriage, leisure and

83

education: the educational opportunities available for people with certain characteristics and the occupations that follow from these opportunities; and the way to find this kind of material, including local sources. The game is played in teams of from two to four people and each team is given a case history of an imaginary person; they then have to plan his schedule of activities during a typical week. Each round of the game represents one year in the life of this person. The player has to choose activities in the way that he thinks will give the person greatest satisfaction now and yet help him best live a full life in the future. The activities include full-time education, employment, family responsibility, etc. and as each involves some investment of time, money, preparation and training, it is impossible to participate in all of them. Practice is also given in the mechanics of bureaucracy because some activities involve form-filling.

When players have made their decisions scores are totalled in four areas: education, occupation, family life, and leisure. The calculators use tables and spinners based on the US Census, and there is a 'luck' factor built in by the use of spinners and dice. The game runs for a prescribed number of rounds and the team with the highest score at the end wins the game.

This is one of the few games for which an evaluation study has been attempted [3] and the conclusions reached indicate that it has high motivating effects, that the environment it provides is sufficiently realistic to enable players to make decisions in the areas of education, leisure, family life, and occupation, and that it can communicate information of a factual nature. The designer sees its prime use as the centre-piece of a package which contains material for vocational testing, supplementary reading, expanded role-playing of some of the situations built into the game, and filmed materials.

ii *Communal Living*. The game of DEMOCRACY has been evolved by Professor James S. Coleman as an aid to adolescents in learning about the society they live in. It is composed of eight games which simulate the legislative process. Players in the basic game act as representatives of the people: they are given cards which indicate their constituents' feelings on some of the issues which come before the legislature. Their success as representatives is measured by the number of Bills supported by their constituents that they manage to get through, and the number that their constituents do not favour that they get rejected. It is a complex game to explain but the rules are clear and precisely defined. The game is played by from six to eleven players and takes from thirty minutes to four hours depending on how many of the games are played. A single copy costs one dollar fifty cents and it could easily be adapted to suit British conditions and children. The authors have used the original version in schools and found the children interested in it as a game, even though it is USA-oriented.

Other games using the same basic scenario are NAPOLI from the Western Behavioral Sciences Institute which seems to be almost identical to DEMOCRACY, and SECTION, a game devised by Abt Associates for the High Schools Geography Project. In this latter game the players are members of conflicting groups in an imaginary part of the USA. The action takes place just before the meeting of the State Legislature which will allocate funds for public works. The players compete and co-operate to get these funds.

iii *Geographic Games.* This is the one part of education in this country where a considerable amount of work has been done on academic gaming. The authors were able to track down a number of these through the good offices of J. A. Crisp, Head of Geography at Malory School, Bromley. It is probable that the initial impetus came from J. P. Cole and G. A. Smith of Nottingham University [5]. Games have also been devised by Rex Walford of Maria Grey College, Twickenham. John Everson HMI and Brian Fitzgerald of St. Dunstan's College, Catford, have developed an urban simulation model, 'Dunstanbridge', based on the possible growth of Cambridge, and M. A. Morgan of the Bristol University Department of Geography has produced a simulation model called 'Micropolis' which reproduces the growth of an English country town.

Simulation and gaming in education

iv *Economic Games*. Two games from Johns Hopkins University attempt to present a study of economics at different levels. CONSUMER by Gerald Zaltman performs a worthwhile task in teaching the problems and economics of hire-purchase. Most of the players are purchasers, and there are also salesmen, co-ordinators and hire-purchase firms. The purchasers have a monthly income which they use to buy goods whose cost is constant unless the purchaser has to auction them off in times of credit shortage. Utility points are issued for items bought but these points vary at different times and it is sometimes necessary for the purchaser to borrow money to make purchases and get more of them. He may go to the bank, the hire-purchase company or to the shop to get credit, and players representing these organizations compete with each other for his credit, obtaining points for completed transactions and losing them under certain conditions. There is one salesman whose function is to hold auctions and to disburse items bought. A co-ordinator supervises the general running of the game and acts as judge.

The game is designed to make the purchaser weigh the added cost of credit against the desirability of possessing the article. It also makes him consider if he could spend his money better on other things, and makes him think about the possibility of the occurrence of unexpected events not covered by insurance. Zaltman recommends the game for groups studying problems of democracy, mathematics, home economics, and for integrated courses.

The second game is devised by James S. Coleman and Robert Harris and is called ECONOMIC SYSTEM. It shows players a wide range of economic systems, and concepts taught include the importance of planning and of budgeting. Each player takes one of four economic roles and sells either his labour or a commodity. With the money he receives he must buy the raw materials for his commodity, or articles for personal consumption if he is a worker. The winner of the game is the person who secures for himself the highest standard of living.

It is claimed for this game that in the playing of it the participants learn at first hand some of the things that exist in our economic system. Amongst these are the benefits of co-operation between manufacturers and between sellers, the fact that when the price of one article rises, the prices of other goods rise as well, and other examples of the interdependence of actions.

There are many more games, most of which have originated in America, are designed for American conditions and would need modification before they could be applied here. This modification could probably be done fairly easily, and the games would then be suitable for a wide range of abilities and ages. Tansey and Unwin [8] have produced a list of available games.

BIBLIOGRAPHY

1. ALLEN, LAYMAN E.: *Towards Autotelic Learning of Mathematical Logic.* Mathematics Teacher, 56, Jan. 1963, 8–21.

2. BLOOMFIELD, LINCOLN P. *and* PADELFORD, NORMAN J.: *Three Experiments in Political Gaming.* American Political Science Review, 53, Dec. 1959, 1105–15.

3. BOOCOCK, SARANE S.: *Simulation of a Learning Environment for Career Planning and Vocational Choice.* Paper prepared for the Annual Meeting of the American Psychological Association, Sept. 1966, John Hopkins University, Department of Social Relations. Mimeo.

4. CHERRYHOLMES, CLEO: *Developments in Simulation of International Relations in High School Teaching.* Phi Delta Kappan, 46, Jan. 1965, 227–31.

5. COLE, J. P. *and* SMITH, G. A.: *Geographical Games.* Bulletin of Quantitative Data for Geographers, Nottingham University, Department of Geography, Mar. 1967. Mimeo.

6. GEARON, JOHN D.: *War or Peace: A Simulation Game.* Social Education, 30, Nov. 1966, 521–2.

7. KAPLAN, ALICE J. *and* GORDON, MARTIN S.: *A Critique of War or Peace: A Simulation Game.* Social Education, 31, May 1967, 383–5.

8. TANSEY, P. J. *and* UNWIN, DERICK: *Academic Games Currently Being Marketed.* Bulletins on Academic Gaming and Simulation, Number 5. Bulmershe College of Education, Reading, May 1968.

Simulation and gaming in education
RELATED READING

BERNE, ERIC: *Games People Play.* New York, Grove Press, 1966.

BIDDLE, BRUCE *and* THOMAS, EDWIN J.: *Role Theory, Concepts and Research.* New York, John Wiley, 1966.

GARVEY, DALE M. *and* SEILER, WILLIAM H.: *A Study of the Effectiveness of Different Methods of Teaching.* Emporia, Kansas State Teachers' College, 1966. Mimeo.

GIFFIN, SIDNEY F.: *The Crisis Game: Simulating International Conflict.* New York, Doubleday, 1965.

HERMAN, CHARLES F. *and* HERMAN, MARGARET G.: *An attempt to Simulate the Start of World War One.* American Political Science Review, 61, June 1967, 400–16.

INBAR, MICHAEL: *The Differential Impact of a Game Simulating a Community Disaster.* American Behavioral Scientist, 10, Oct. 1966, 18–27.

WEALE, W. BRUCE: *The Usefulness of Business Games.* Atlanta Economic Review, Oct. 1963.

WING, RICHARD: *Computer Based Economics Games.* Audiovisual Instruction, 9, Dec. 1964, 681–2.

CHAPTER SIX

Simulation in the classroom

Physicists have their ripple tanks, geographers have their wave-form tanks and little children have their dolls and toy soldiers. Simulation is within the experience of each one of us. It is not even a new concept in the classroom in some of its forms. What is new, possibly, is the realization of the potential of the technique as an aid in education.

The method has value wherever the environmental or working conditions are too difficult or costly to reproduce, or are so complex that they are difficult to understand, or are too dangerous. This last condition was the reason why simulation was first used as a military training technique, but if it has any validity in the classroom, it is probably only valid in craft workshops and results in working models which can be defined as static simulations and which do not concern us. We are concerned both with expense and with complexity and a lot of the work that can be done in a classroom is aimed at the simplification of problems, and can be presented quite cheaply both as far as money is concerned, and at least as importantly, as far as teacher effort is concerned.

Although simulation may well be used in selection and in assessment, the classroom is not the place, at the present time,

for such uses. It could well be that in the future and in association with Industrial Training Boards, simulations could be set
up to measure a pupil's potential ability for a specific appren-
ticeship. When this time comes it is fairly certain that simulation will be found to be a better instrument for selection than
the interview. At least it can be made far less subjective.
When it is used as a device for assessment its chief use is to
measure deviations from the norm, and more will be said
about this aspect of simulation when its use in pre-service
teacher training is discussed in the next chapter.

In this chapter we shall be discussing the third principal
function of simulation, namely its ability to instruct, and to
train students either in specific tasks or in attitudes to a
variety of things. As a training device, simulation can be
thought of as having a lot in common with audio-visual aids.
If it is compared with the moving film, it shares with it the
vividness of presentation which arouses interest, but this alone
does not make anything an effective teaching tool: film has
not been particularly well used as an instructional device at
any level of education.

In the same way, because simulation involves children
deeply, and motivates them to work hard during the process,
the authors originally felt that they were necessarily being
instructed at the same time. We have discovered that this was
not always the case. Frequently children were merely being
entertained as they might be at a film shown without preamble.
While it is now accepted that there is not necessarily learning just because there is involvement, it is easy to turn
the involvement to good educational use. It is, after all,
one of the necessary conditions before learning *can* take
place.

The design of a simulation is no different from that of a
game. Let us assume that we have a simulation ready for use in
a classroom, that we are decided about its use and what we
hope it will teach. Now let us consider the fairly common-sense
plan that a simulation might take in a classroom. First there is
a briefing session before play begins. This should not take too
long, otherwise some of the children become bored and the

actual exercise itself might have to be rushed. During this time the teacher structures the simulation: he gives players the roles they have to assume, and tells them the rules. If there are any accessories such as report forms, profiles or play money this is the time to give them out and explain their use in the game. This is also the time to 'set the stage' by describing backgrounds and indicating specific objectives of individuals and the purpose of the game in general terms. It is as well not to answer questions at this stage, but to deal with them as they arise in the course of the game – many questions will answer themselves as the game proceeds. Early questioning is sometimes used by pupils as a tactic which delays the transformation from the passive state of sitting to the active state of doing.

When the students have been told the aims and purpose of the exercise, and they are aware of the means at their disposal for achieving these ends, the actual simulation should begin. The teacher's function during the play will not be a dominating one. He should be available to answer questions that arise in the course of the exercise, to encourage those who need it, to determine the start and finish of periods when there is a division into time sequences, and in general to administer the rules in whatever form they exist. At this stage there will be little need to act as a controller from the point of view of discipline except where the high motivation causes a break down of inhibition on the part of the students. It has been the case in some simulations that players become so involved in their respective roles that voices, and sometimes fists, are raised. We have found that, as soon as the students have realized what is happening, they cheerfully return to normality.

The most important part of any simulation is the analysis that must take place after its conclusion. This is the stage of reinforcement, the time when what has been learned is clearly brought to the notice of the student. If it was a game rather than a simulation the teacher would count up scores at this stage. Simulation might be a better classroom technique than academic gaming because this aspect is missing. When a game is completed, the score may be viewed by the player as the end in itself, and the reason that the game had been played.

91

In an academic game this is a period of unwinding, of relaxation, and general conversations break out between the players. It is difficult to discuss the game in terms other than those which concern the improvement of performance.

This block in the continuity of the learning process does not occur where there is no fixed scoring system. That is when the element of competition is subordinate to the element of co-operation. It seems that there are marked advantages in any educational process which stresses this co-operative element in our society. Competition is an aspect of our society which schools have emphasized too much in the past. Competition can very often lead to disappointment and loss of dignity: co-operation cannot do so in itself.

During this post-play period of a simulation, the main function of the teacher-controller is to shape and direct the discussion of the way the game has developed. In the simulation decisions have to be taken. In the discussion two questions seem to be important: why were they taken and what were their effects? The purpose of simulating real life situations is so that participants can feel themselves to be a part of the situation, more able to handle the situation if it arises or more tolerant when it does. To help them in this, it is necessary for transfer of training actually to take place. It is no use hoping that it will, as we have done as a justification for teaching Euclidean geometry for hundreds of years. We must help it to happen, we must ask questions. What did players learn from the simulation? If it is not clear, then at this stage they must be helped to discover or to express what their involvement actually means in the real life situation. What frustrations, or constraints, did they feel? These frustrations are felt by people in the real situation. How do they overcome them? How would they change their actions if they were to participate on another occasion? They should also be asked to justify their decisions, to decide if they were made on emotive or on rational grounds.

If this analysis is done, then the best judges of the simulation are the participants. They will know and tell you whether they think it is a possible or probable situation. By knowing how they feel about it, they will give you the best measure of its effectiveness. If there is any need to modify it, this will become evident in these discussions, as indeed will the places where the modifying is required. On all early runs of a simulation, you will discover places where it has to be changed, but this does not mean it has been ineffective. When a participant has thought about a simulation enough to suggest where it should be changed, he cannot but have learned from it. What he has learned may not be explicit, but so much in education at any level is implicit anyway.

The person on the shop floor of education has seen many educational innovations in his time as a practical teacher, and has been willing, at least initially, to try most of them. He has also been forced to the conclusion quite often that there is something wrong with all of them. In visual aids he has been dependent on other people to make the aids, for not many teachers can find the money or the time to make, for example, their own films or film strips. Once a teacher depends on some other person he finds that what he is offered is seldom exactly tailored to his needs. The film strip with twenty frames has only ten at the most which he can use, the film or television takes him where he did not want to go. The television goes too fast for some of the class, or the producer has ideas at variance with what the teacher wants. The teaching machine gathers dust because there are far too few programmes published for it.

Now simulation has a case for use *in the schools* only if it is relatively inexpensive, if it does not use up too much of a teacher's time, if it is widely applicable – does not have to be rewritten for each age and ability group – and, most important, if it leaves the teacher with a great deal of freedom to act as freely as has long been his right. Not all simulation situations can qualify as fulfilling all these conditions. For instance simulators are used as procedure trainers. A person in a school might learn to drive using a simulator. Here also a skill is being taught and there is a right and several wrong ways. There is no freedom of choice here. Again, cathode ray tubes, thermometers, and other signalling devices may be used to simulate and to train the perceptions and there would naturally

93

be rigidity in their use, but these devices are being used to condition; the things they teach are clear, non-controversial, and offer few if any alternatives.

When values are being shaped, decisions are being made, and situations that are not rule-bound are under discussion, education performs its true function. This is the situation in the average classroom in which children are being educated in Britain today. Here, simulation offers the teacher freedom to decide on the content. It is not wasteful of his time, and is fluid enough to be adaptable to suit a variety of age, ability and interest groups.

It seems most likely that the principal techniques used in simulation studies in the classroom will be case studies and role-playing situations. Consider a practical example of one of these. One of the authors has a group of students learning these techniques as an educational study option for a period of four hours per week. They are second year pre-service teachers, and the option begins in their sixth term of training. They had had only four hours of simulation training when another member of staff asked them to prepare a simulation for use in a weekend workshop at a leading public school. The concern was with situations that would involve a group of the schoolboys aged between fifteen and seventeen in decision making. The course started the next day, and the students were asked not only to devise, but to present situations in a form that could be immediately used. Three simulations were prepared by the fourteen students divided into two groups of four and one group of six working independently. Each group had finished its simulation, and had presented it on master duplicating sheets ready for reproduction within four hours of class time. Even though the students had had virtually no training, their performance was an excellent one and the workshop was a success.

Let us take a closer look at the situation prepared by the group of six. The others are not included because of shortage of space, but they are at least as good as this one.

The subject of the simulation that is set out here is an interview for the post of youth club leader. The subject matter

of this simulation was arrived at without our help, and this
was particularly interesting because we had had the opportunity to see a similar thing done at the simulation training
weekend course in Salisbury mentioned earlier in this volume.
The exercise is shown below in the form that it was presented
at the workshop. It consists of six completed application
forms, a copy of each being given to all members of the selection
panel, and the appropriate one to each of the people who are
playing the roles of applicant. There is a single reference for
each of the applicants, and background information about
each of the candidates. Suggested incidents which could occur
during the interview are also included.

The purpose of the present exercise was a consideration of
the moral aspects of 'choice'. The pages that follow show what
students were able to achieve in some four hours working time.

SIMULATION EXERCISE INTERVIEW

An aspect of choice

PREPARED BY   Denis Barber, Richard Craft, John Goodwin
John Gosling, Peter Morrison and Mike
Wilkinson,
Students of Bulmershe College of Education,
1968.

In this simulation exercise applications have been invited for the job of youth leader at Dowling New Town, Sussex.

Six applications have been received for the post. It has been decided to interview three of these, and a short list has first to be prepared. It is assumed that one of the candidates will be offered the post. There are three distinct phases in the exercise, which is designed for a group of six participants.

The kit contains:

Phase 1:   six application forms.

Phase 2: a   the application forms of the three candidates who have been short-listed;

       b   background information relating to each of these three candidates.

Phase 3: a   application forms;

       b   background information for interviewing board;

       c   references of candidates;

       d   incident slips which are held by the controller and issued from time to time during the course of the interview.

DIRECTIONS

Phase 1:   All six boys act as individual selectors, and each must make a short list of three candidates from the six applicants. They are to state on the forms provided their reasons for choosing each of their three selections and also their reasons for rejecting the other three. (These forms, which are not shown here, merely contain the names of the candidates at intervals of one third of a page. The space between is used for notes on each during this initial phase.)

This is a convenient stopping point if time is pressing, and the reasons for the various choices can be discussed. If, however, there is no need to terminate the exercise at this point, it can proceed without pause to . . .

Phase 2: The group splits up as follows.

   i. The three candidates selected for interview. At this point three of the boys will assume the roles of these three applicants.

  ii. Two other boys who will act as interviewers. They must decide on the type of question, and even on specific questions that they will ask the candidates during the interview. These questions must be designed to help investigate background information and also be relevant to information given on the application forms.

 iii. A director who will control the whole procedure from now onwards.

Phase 3: The interview itself. The director is in charge of this. The interview room should be separate from the waiting room so that candidates cannot hear what has gone on in the interviews of other candidates. From time to time the director will pass a note to either a member of the interviewing board or to the candidate being interviewed telling him to take a certain action. (Examples of these are given later.) He can either use the slips provided or make up his own incidents, and some of these may well be the results of something said during the interview.

Both candidates and interviewers should be shown relative background information before Phase 3 starts in order that the questions asked and the answers will be relevant.

APPLICATION FORM

NAME	Christine Rhodes
DATE OF BIRTH	17th September 1920. AGE 47 years
NATIONALITY	British
PLACE OF BIRTH	Bristol, England
PRESENT ADDRESS	16 Acacia Avenue, Dowling New Town, Sussex
OTHER ADDRESSES	None
STATUS	Single
NUMBER OF CHILDREN	None
AGE / SEX OF CHILDREN	N/A
PRESENT OCCUPATION	Matron, Redlands Hospital
PREVIOUS EMPLOYMENT	As a nurse in various hospitals
EDUCATION	Raedon Girls' School, 1931–37 Durham University 1938–42. (Honours degree Zoology.)
RELIGION	Church of England
INTERESTS / HOBBIES	Welfare work, archery
PERSONAL DETAILS	*Previous illnesses :* none

REASONS FOR APPLICATION

After spending twenty-five years in hospital service, I have now reached the peak of my career. However, I feel that I have still plenty to offer in the field of youth work. I therefore apply for the post of youth leader certain that I can fulfil the duties expected of me. I am, as you can imagine, knowledgeable on all medical matters concerning children and young people. I also hold awards for the coaching of archery, rounders, and cricket. If appointed I would be prepared to take a drop in salary as I feel that I could really enjoy this kind of activity.

APPLICATION FORM

NAME	Knight, Edward Peter
DATE OF BIRTH	19th April, 1927. AGE 41 years
NATIONALITY	British
PLACE OF BIRTH	Sherborne, Dorset
PRESENT ADDRESS	5 Silvery Mews, South Kensington
OTHER ADDRESSES	River Mansions, Newbury, Berks.
STATUS	Single
NUMBER OF CHILDREN	None
AGE / SEX OF CHILDREN	N/A
PRESENT OCCUPATION	Managing Director, Southlakes Estates Corporation Ltd.
PREVIOUS EMPLOYMENT	Director on Boards of various companies
EDUCATION	Sherborne School, Sherborne, Dorset. Cambridge University
RELIGION	Roman Catholic
INTERESTS / HOBBIES	Water skiing, motor racing, horse riding, tennis, scoutmaster
PERSONAL DETAILS	*Previous illnesses:* T.B. 1941–47. Now no trace.

REASONS FOR APPLICATION

I have been very interested in young people all my life. Having succeeded in business, I would now like to apply my talents to helping boys and young people to make the best of their lives. Since I am used to organising groups of people, I am convinced that I would be useful on the administrative side as well as in direct contact with young people. I feel that I can offer a wealth of experience of the world combined with a genuine concern for the welfare of young people. In the past I have been in the fortunate position of being able to help local youth movements financially, and my company has recently built, at its own expense, a new youth wing at the Basentake Community Centre. I am aware that this position does not pay a salary equivalent to my present emolument, but as I am a director I will still receive part of my salary without being required to attend the office constantly or even frequently.

APPLICATION FORM

NAME	George Flynn
DATE OF BIRTH	6th May 1933. AGE 35 years
NATIONALITY	Irish
PLACE OF BIRTH	Cork
PRESENT ADDRESS	26 Border Avenue, Winborough
OTHER ADDRESSES	None
STATUS	Married, June 15th 1956
NUMBER OF CHILDREN	Three
AGE / SEX OF CHILDREN	Boy, 10; girl, 9; boy 3
PRESENT OCCUPATION	Football manager
PREVIOUS EMPLOYMENT	Went straight from school into professional soccer with Cork Corinthians, and in 1952 was transferred to Newbridge United with whom I played for ten years. I also played for Bradford, Grimsby Town and Hereford before becoming player-manager to Winborough Town last year.
EDUCATION	West Cork High School
RELIGION	Roman Catholic
INTERESTS / HOBBIES	Outdoor pursuits, travelling
PERSONAL DETAILS	*Previous illnesses:* pneumonia at eight years. Broken femur twice since 1963.

REASONS FOR APPLICATION

After a football career that has spanned twenty-two years, and having represented my country over thirty times, fifteen as captain, I feel that now my playing days are over, I could easily devote myself to the youth organization. I have qualities of leadership as is indicated by my being captain of both an international and club soccer sides and manager of Winborough Town and I think that this will be invaluable in the job you are offering. When I was with Newbridge I ran coaching courses for youngsters which were well attended and this was repeated at Bradford. As you can see from my application form, I am interested in outdoor pursuits and the knowledge I have gained from these during my travels around the world would be of great assistance to the youngsters. Whilst at Grimsby I was connected with two youth clubs and I used to run courses at the local grammar school. I also ran a club in Winborough. I think my connection with children over the past ten years coupled with my ability to organize would stand me in good stead for the job. Finally, at 35, I would like a job with security.

APPLICATION FORM

NAME	William K. George
DATE OF BIRTH	4th October, 1943. AGE 24 years
NATIONALITY	British
PLACE OF BIRTH	Kingston, Jamaica
PRESENT ADDRESS	7 North Road, Woodley, Berks.
OTHER ADDRESSES	None
STATUS	Single
NUMBER OF CHILDREN	None
AGE / SEX OF CHILDREN	N/A
PRESENT OCCUPATION	Bus driver
PREVIOUS EMPLOYMENT	I have just graduated from university
EDUCATION	Kingston Boys' School Reading University
RELIGION	Humanist
INTERESTS / HOBBIES	All sports, music and the arts. I have recently helped to run the Woodley Youth Club.
PERSONAL DETAILS	*Previous illnesses:* none apart from the usual childhood diseases.

REASONS FOR APPLICATION

Until recently I was not absolutely sure that I was suitable for work in the youth movement, but my recent experience in helping to run the Woodley Youth Centre has shown me that this is the sort of work that I would like to do. My knowledge of sociology convinces me that there is a great deal to be done in this field. This, together with my interests in sport and music and the arts generally, convinces me that I have a lot to offer both as an instructor and as an administrator.

APPLICATION FORM

NAME   Dereck Ayram

DATE OF BIRTH   17th February, 1937. AGE 31 years

NATIONALITY   British

PLACE OF BIRTH   Ilkeston, Derbyshire

PRESENT ADDRESS   24 Clifftop Drive, Shrimpton, Kent

OTHER ADDRESSES   None

STATUS   Married

NUMBER OF CHILDREN   Two

AGE / SEX OF CHILDREN   Girl aged six, boy aged four

PRESENT OCCUPATION   Prison warder

PREVIOUS EMPLOYMENT   None

EDUCATION   St. Margaret's County Grammar School
Social Welfare course (one year)

RELIGION   Church of England

PERSONAL DETAILS   *Previous illnesses:* caught malaria while on National Service.

REASONS FOR APPLICATION

After being a prison warder for the past ten years, I feel that I have all of the necessary experience for dealing with all kinds of people. In prison I have to organize the prisoners socially and feel that after dealing with hardened criminals I will be able to look after children very capably. I have two children of my own and am very interested in what children like to do. If I get the job, I shall endeavour to carry on my social work with the children without imposing the restrictions of prison life.

APPLICATION FORM

NAME	Peter James McCormack
DATE OF BIRTH	17th May 1935. AGE 33 years.
NATIONALITY	Scottish
PLACE OF BIRTH	Glasgow
PRESENT ADDRESS	35 Christmas Drive, Kettering,
OTHER ADDRESSES	None
STATUS	Single
NUMBER OF CHILDREN	None
AGE / SEX OF CHILDREN	N/A
PRESENT OCCUPATION	Secondary school P.E. teacher
PREVIOUS EMPLOYMENT	None
EDUCATION	Kettering High School
	Loughborough College of Physical Education
RELIGION	Presbyterian
INTERESTS / HOBBIES	All forms of sport with particular emphasis on team games, cycling, coin collecting, writing.
PERSONAL DETAILS	*Previous illnesses:* Asthma as a young child but this cleared up in my late teens.

REASONS FOR APPLICATION

I have always been extremely interested in children and their development, this being the reason that I entered the teaching profession. Because of my keen interest in sport I became a teacher of physical education.

Because I have been teaching for twelve years, I felt that I would like to change my job, although I should like to remain with children, offering them the valuable experience I have gained over the years as a teacher. The youth service seems to offer such an opportunity for me.

If I am selected for the job I will arrange as many worthwhile activities and pursuits as possible, both physical and social, in an endeavour to contribute to the shaping of children's characters.

My experiences as a teacher gave me plenty of opportunities for organizational and administrative experiences, both of which are essential parts of the post you are offering. I would endeavour to make the Centre as interesting, informal and friendly as possible if I am offered the post, and would try to help the children develop socially to the best of my ability.

REFERENCES

These have been put in one list to save space, but should be separated for use in the exercise.

1. *Reference for George Flynn*

While he was with Newbridge United, I found George Flynn a most reliable and punctual person. His organization of the coaching course was very good and he was a most valuable member of our team both on and off the field. As a leader he was excellent, and brought many honours both to himself and to the team.

F. D. Wheeler,
Chairman,
Newbridge United F.C.

2. *Reference for Dereck Ayram*

Dereck Ayram has always been a steady worker and has been invaluable in organizing social events within the prison. He is liked by the prisoners and has always got on well with them.

H. C. Lee,
Governor,
Shrimpton Prison.

3. *Reference for Christine Rhodes*

I found Miss Rhodes to be an excellent person during her ten years with me. She is a good disciplinarian and is extremely knowledgeable on medical matters. I would strongly recommend her to any prospective employer.

H. C. Caine, M.B., Ch.B.
Surgical Registrar,
Redlands Hospital.

4. *Reference for William K. George*

William is a hard working and industrious person. His course here was thoroughly successful and we were pleased with his examination results. He contributed over his three years both
104

in the field of sport and drama. I hope that he will use his degree to the best advantage.

T. Boulter, M.A. (Oxon)
Dean,
Faculty of Letters,
Reading University.

5. *Reference for Peter McCormack*

Mr. McCormack is an extremely conscientious teacher who has established excellent relationships with both pupils and staff. He is a first class administrator and an excellent organizer and his school teams have achieved both good results and enviable reputations for sportsmanship and conduct. This is a direct result of his enthusiasm and guidance. I have no hesitation in recommending him for any work connected with children and young people.

P. M. Chrysler,
Headmaster.

6. *Reference for Edward Peter Knight*

I have known Mr. Knight for twelve years, both socially and as a business colleague. During this time I have been very impressed with his integrity and great ability which is displayed in everything he undertakes.

I am sure that he would be of great value to your organization.

Geo. Brown,
General Manager,
Alliance Property Holdings Ltd.

INTERVIEW   PHASE 3: *Suggested Questions for Interviewers*

1. What are your views on drinking? Would you consider having a licensed bar on the club premises for use of the over 18s?
2. How close a link would you wish between your church and the club?

3. Suppose that a youth who had just returned from a reform school asked to join your club, and he was a convicted thief, would you allow him to do so?

4. How would you deal with members who did not want to take part in club activities but just spent their time drinking coffee while they were at the club? It is not suggested that they cause any trouble.

INTERVIEW   PHASE 3: *Background Information*

Dereck Ayram: Cleared of a charge of assault brought by a prisoner in 1960.

Christine Rhodes: While at university she was a member of the Communist Party and was widely known for her radical views.

George Flynn: He was accused in a Sunday paper of having accepted bribes to lose matches while on the staff of Newbridge United. He was actually charged with this offence but was not convicted and sued the paper for libel successfully. Three of the team were convicted at this time and he left the club soon after.

Peter McCormack: On one occasion when he was a young teacher he beat a boy rather severely. There was trouble with the parents and he left the school.

William George: Last week he was convicted of careless driving and had his licence endorsed.

Edward Knight: His wife has filed a petition for divorce on the grounds of desertion but no court hearing has taken place yet.

INTERVIEW   PHASE 3: *Incidents*

a. Ask Knight if his wife will be living in the district or if he will be travelling to the Centre from his present address.

b. Ask Flynn which Sunday papers he reads.

c. Knock book on to floor between each candidate and the table.

d. Talk, or rather ask one question, in a low voice so that the candidate has difficulty in hearing.

Ask each candidate a. to attempt a mechanical puzzle,

                               b. to make the next move in a chess game

                               c. to solve a crossword clue

and express mild surprise if he is unable to do any of these things.

APPENDIX

A brief report on the simulation by Mr. Tim Newell-Price, principal lecturer and head of the Religious Education Department at Bulmershe College of Education who commissioned the simulation and conducted the workshop.

The participants were a group of seven youths whose ages ranged from 15 to 17+. The simulation was part of a workshop on CHOICE as an aspect of moral behaviour.

PHASE 1. This was taken as it stood with the seven participants taking the forms and putting the candidates in their own order of preference. They were then asked to give reasons for their choice and an interesting and wide ranging discussion resulted. The short list consisted of George, Flynn and McCormack and the person finally chosen was McCormack.

At the interview were the three candidates, the other four youths in the group (who took the roles of the interviewing panel with one of their members elected as chairman) and a Marlborough College staff member acting as Youth Services Director. All of the panel had copies of the background information of each candidate, but the candidates had information about nobody but themselves. The incident sheet was held by the Director and the question sheet was kept by the chairman of the interviewing panel.

The simulation took two hours and a half but it could have been continued longer.

Remember that this example was prepared in four hours by second year students who had very little experience. Certainly they were extremely good students, but they have shown clearly that simulation is a viable teaching method at the present time. Such simulations could well be quickly organized by groups of teachers meeting at Teachers' Centres. They would seem to be extremely applicable in integrated humanities courses and for senior pupils, especially the average and less able groups.

Clearly, this simulation is not a smooth and polished one, but it worked, and it worked with a group that one might expect to be more sophisticated than the average person of their age would be. This would seem to indicate that the high degree of involvement engendered by the simulation permits participants to overlook its defects. On the other hand there is a vast amount of material in this simulation available for discussion, not only at the time, but at a later date.

The simulation could have been improved by giving roles to the members of the interviewing panel and by increasing the background information about each of the candidates to include his strengths as well as apparent weaknesses. The design of the simulation in groups of six is good in that five or more teams can play and results can then be compared at the end. Also the phasing of play permits a straight run through or suitable breaks to coincide with lesson bells.

Other simulations have been attempted in the United States of America. A management of resources game has been described by Christine [1]; the HSGP [2] have devised a simulation called Metfab in which a site for a new factory has to be located and Gearon [3] has written of a labour *versus* management game. Teachers at El Capitan High school, Lakeside, California have compiled a simulation which is based in the post-holocaust period after the bomb has been dropped and during an invasion from outer space.

There are many other examples of successful simulations in existence ranging over a wide field both as regards subject and time. They are so easy to arrange that it should be possible for any group of teachers to arrange their own.

BIBLIOGRAPHY

1. CHRISTINE, CHARLES *and* CHRISTINE, DOROTHY: *Simulation, a Teaching Tool.* Elementary School Journal, 67, May 1967, 396–8.
2. *High Schools Geography Project Newsletter,* No. 15. May 1968, HSGP, P.O. Box 1095, Boulder, Colorado 80302.
3. GEARON, JOHN D.: *Labour vs Management: A Simulation Game.* Social Education, 30, Oct. 1966, 421–2.

RELATED READING

ANTRIM, W. H.: *Realistic Learning in a Simulated Environment.* American Vocational Journal, 42, Jan. 1967, 29–31.

CHERRYHOLMES, CLEO: *Development of Simulation of International Relations in High School Teaching.* Phi Delta Kappan, 46, Jan. 1965, 227–31.

GARVEY, DALE M. *and* SEILER, W. H.: *On Simulation Teaching.* Phi Delta Kappan, 69, Apr. 1968, 473.

GUETZKOW, HAROLD: *A use of Simulation in the Study of Inter-Nation Relations.* Behavioral Science, 4, 1959, 183–91.

GUSS, C.: *Role Playing Simulation in Instruction.* Audiovisual Instruction, 11, June 1966, 443–4.

KOHN, CLYDE F.: *Selected Classroom Experiences.* High School Geography Project (Geographic Education Series No. 4). Publication Center, National Council for Geographic Education, Illinois State Normal University, Normal, Illinois, 1964.

SPRAGUE, HALL T. *and* SHIRTS, GARY: *Exploring Classroom Uses of Simulation.* Western Behavioral Sciences Institute, Oct. 1966, Mimeo.

CHAPTER SEVEN

Simulation in teacher training

The single thing that most people can agree about in the education system of the British Isles today is that it is divisive. Many are the ingenious ways of separating the sheep from the goats. There is the systematic hierarchy of the public school, the direct grant grammar school, the grammar school, the comprehensive school, the multilateral, the bilateral, the secondary modern and, of course, the private school whose place is uncertain and whose quality is equally hard to determine. There is the division into streams and sets; into academic and non-academic groups within the schools; the division into vocational and academic courses. And all the while there is the great division between the theory and the practice of education.

In schools the tendency is to divide pupils on the basis of an arbitrarily selected attribute which we call intelligence, and measure people on the basis of their possession of little or much of this attribute. There are those in education who think that this is not right; who feel that competition is not the central theme of life, nor is content the measure of education. The people who see society as a whole, a unit, are the ones who try to change the system, who favour *truly* comprehensive schools, and who are the theorists in education. They are often condemned for this and stand accused of being too far away from the shop floor of education where their theories have to be carried out. This is a charge frequently laid at the door of colleges of education.

It is claimed by the critics of colleges that they are too theoretically based, that their students do not get enough time in the classroom actually practising the art of teaching, and that much of what students are taught has little direct relevance in the classroom. A good deal of this criticism may seem to be justified, but only if we take a superficial view of the teacher's roles. Would anyone expect a doctor to be efficient without a background study of those sciences that are basic to medicine? And are not sociology, psychology, philosophy, history of education and comparative education the bases of the practice of education? If this is so, and if the teaching service warrants the status of *profession* then surely the teaching of these background disciplines is fundamental and necessary. Again, many teachers are old, and long in the service. They have no experience of colleges of education but remember, with the enchantment of distance, the old training colleges with their readily available 'Tips for Teachers'.

It could be that colleges of education have gone too far away from this practical approach. Perhaps the aim of turning out a finished product from the training college was a good one, though the finished product might never read another book concerned with education in forty years of classroom practice. But even if we sought to increase the practical content of today's courses there are difficulties in reaching a balance between theory and practice. This is particularly true for those teachers who are training for the secondary age range. Consider the situation of a headmaster of a secondary school in the urban South-East of England. He will receive students from a local college of education at least twice a year for periods of up to a term. Then the local university department of education will want to use his school for students during the whole of the spring term, and there are specialist and 'wing' colleges who will wish to send him students who are

111

studying such diverse things as Home Science and Physical Education. Apart from this he will have requests from individual lecturers to let him bring students in for a day, or one day per week, or some such thing for some specific purpose. With the best will in the world, he must, at some stage say 'no more'. Teachers who are constantly under student pressure tire of it, parents expect continuity of teaching for their children, and life can be intolerable when a bad student arrives. But students do not get enough time in the schools: they maintain that this is so, and lecturers are aware of it. Yet there is a stalemate because there just are not places in the schools to accommodate all the people we are training.

It is necessary in these circumstances, if we wish to relate the theory of teaching with its practice, to search for an alternative to visits to an actual classroom. We must apply the theory of teaching to the classroom and try to relate the two within the confines of the *college* if it cannot be done in the schools. To do this we should first decide what the students need to know, and then consider how to present this knowledge to them in a way that will be both realistic and relevant.

Simulation seems to offer this alternative, and it is finding more and more acceptance, especially overseas, as a way of compensating students under training for lack of actual time spent in practice. It has often been postulated that a college of education course enables a student to be aware of educational theories, to be able to talk about education, but not to be familiar with the individuality of the children that make up any group. Efforts are made to overcome this deficiency: observation of classes is carried out, groups of students go into classrooms with individual teachers for group practices, and children are brought into the college and used in demonstrations. All of these things are good, but the students do not feel that they are enough. In the training of teachers what is needed is something that will bridge the gap between theory and practice; between the way we talk about the job and the way it is done; between verbal commitment and actual behaviour.

In the lecture, tutorial, or seminar situation where the
112

student is learning the methodology of the classroom situation, the context of learning is not the context in which the knowledge will have to be applied. This is an incompatibility which is much more than a physical one, and makes it difficult for the trainee to relate what is said in these circumstances to the situation that exists when he is in the classroom actually teaching. It is this as much as anything that causes the charge of excessive theorizing to be laid at the doors of colleges of education. Recognizing these defects of the system, educationists have searched for a way of bringing the situation of the classroom into the college, and as early as 1950 Jacobs [2] was writing about 'sociodrama' in the training of teachers. He writes:

> . . . the dynamics of the human relationships involved in solving problems of common interest through conjoint effort with others – an almost daily occurrence in the activities of a teacher – can be understood, emphatically, only if the trainee is placed in the real life roles related to such behaviour.

He urges that these real life roles should be brought into the lecture room in order that the student should understand both the dynamics of the situation that he is to study and the effect that his reaction to situations will have on others. In Jacobs' eyes the possibilities of this new method that he advocates are twofold. First they give the student an opportunity to gain an insight into his roles as a teacher in a situation that permits these roles to be viewed relative to others. Secondly it gives him an opportunity of trying out new behaviour patterns, of having a try at something new, in an atmosphere where there is no punishment for making a mistake.

Of course the sociodrama that Jacobs discusses is not quite the same as simulation as it has come to be understood since. For him the drama was the important part: he was concerned that his students should have the chance of acting out the situations in a spontaneous way with no prepared script. Simulation in this context is more concerned with the analysing of the individual's function as a group member. It is argued that group interaction is the important element in personal

113

relationships and that this method allows the student to discover how he reacts to the group and the effects of this reaction on the other members of the group.

It is probable that there is an impulsive need to be, if not liked, at least understood, and this is the basis of the idea of sociodrama. In common with simulation it has the advantages of self-involvement, it permits errors to be made without criticism, it permits the rehearsal of real life situations in order that the rehearser is better prepared when they arise, and it introduces the dynamics of the classroom into the lecture room. Where it differs from simulation is in the high value it places on spontaneity as opposed to structure and its dominating belief in the individual submerged in the group.

The trouble with sociodrama seems to be that it does not go far enough. In an unstructured situation it is possible to say to a student, 'Play the part of a below-average child being disobedient in the classroom', but not to say, 'Here is Tom Wilson, a below average child with the following background, who is misbehaving in your classroom, how are you going to deal with the situation, and why?' Although a teacher is a member of a group, and although his actions are determined by his *role set*, these are fixed in a given situation but vary as situations change. The only constant factor in any individual's role set is the individual. It seems then that the only action that it is possible to discuss and modify is *individual* action. Further, it seems that the fundamental criticism of the lecture system remains a basic criticism of the method of sociodrama. This is that it is non-specific, and only permits the participants to talk about education and hardly helps in the understanding of specific people. While it may cause involvement, it does little to meet the charge that method courses in colleges of education need to be more practical and to deal with reality.

To cope with this problem, the concept of simulation has been developed. Apart from the early approaches to it in the form of sociodrama, simulation in teacher training has followed two main lines. The first method is that of the *role-play* situation. While this is similar to sociodrama, it is far more structured and is in most cases not high in dramatic content.

114

In the typical role-play situation, the participant is given a great deal of information about the background conditions of a school, a class and the community that it serves. He is then asked to play the part of a young teacher who finds himself in the position of teaching the class whose background information he has available to him. There are variations of this. He may, for instance, be given the case history of one child in very great detail and then be asked to explain certain things that occur in the light of this case history.

The other technique that is used in simulation is the *'in-basket technique'*. This method presents a series of situations which might typically occur in the day of a teacher. Usually about twenty items are selected to make up a single 'in-basket' and the exercise is completed when the participant has dealt with them, usually but not necessarily in writing. The case study is not in itself a technique of simulation because it is static while simulation is dynamic, calling for action and reaction. It is one of the props on which simulations are built. Case studies can exist without simulation: their use can be abstract and theoretical and they do not in themselves cause involvement in role.

In-baskets do not need to be written records. It is true that they frequently are, but this is because the written record is the cheapest way of conveying information. Items may be presented as tape recordings, and 'staff meetings', 'interviews with parents', and background noises indicative of such things as lack of control may be best presented in this way, though these are difficult to record. It is difficult to get effective background noise without first class equipment and good operators.

Other devices that can be used in in-baskets are film slides and moving film. At a later stage we shall see how a group of researchers in America use film almost exclusively in their simulation exercises. In general it is a costly process unless it is possible to use a piece of film made for another purpose in conjunction with the simulation exercise. Film slides are much less costly at something over a shilling each, and may be worth while if a striking visual impact is desired. Finally, role-playing can be used in conjunction with the in-basket: the angry parent or the headmaster may appear, or some other unexpected item such as a voice raised in anger outside the door.

The 'normal' simulation employs all the techniques that are necessary or available, but first one needs to decide on problems and situations. Before a simulation is set up, the designer needs to ask what is a typical classroom problem, and how might it be solved. Frequently at this stage it is valuable to discuss the situation with colleagues to get a variety of suggestions and viewpoints. If the designer were to ask a number of teachers how they would handle disciplinary problems, there would be no universal agreement. One man might say that he had used corporal punishment right from the start; another teacher might have found shouting effective; a third might have found that the children ultimately responded to being treated with dignity, or humour, and so it goes.

But this is not all the analysis that is needed to simulate a discipline problem. If such a situation arises, it does not remain static. It either spreads or it ceases to be a problem because it has been brought under control. The designer must find out or think out the methods of bringing disorder under control. Let us assume that a child is misbehaving on one side of the room and an inexperienced teacher sees him, what should he do? Should he shout so that other members of the class are aware of the misdemeanour, or should he move close to the pupil and try to exercise control without involving others? Is there any place for the voice raised above the din calling 'quiet please, everybody'?

It might be helpful at this stage to see how simulation is being used in the training of teachers. The Oregon State System of Higher Education has established a 'Center for Research on Teaching' at Monmouth, Oregon, and work is proceeding on teacher training using simulation of classroom situations.

The project is directed by Paul Twelker and the simulator is the responsibility of Bert Kersh [3]. There are three in-
116

baskets each consisting of twenty items on film. The filmed situation centres round a group of twelve-year-old children in what is called 'Mr. Land's sixth grade classroom'. The participant is a young teacher who has come to observe and to assist with the class. The time of day and the lead into an incident might be given in one of these sequences . . .

MR. LAND'S *Sixth Grade:*

Instruction Procedures.	Teaching Research Division
Program 1 – 1	Monmouth, Oregon
Communication Problem:	March 1965.

Situation: This is the first part of the day, just a few minutes before the tardy bell rings. Mr. Land has been called to the office to straighten out a matter concerning lunch tickets and has asked you to monitor the class. You are standing in front of the room. About half the youngsters are in the room. The rest are coming in from the playground.

Problem Scene: Scene opens on class about half empty. Jack approaches T (trainee) and says that he has been sick the previous week and should not be required to play during recess.

Hold Cue: '. . . to play today.'

RESPONSE METHOD

Standards
  I. In situations involving rules of procedure when the student is not informed of the rules, defer to authority *v* establish own rules.
 II. Show supporting manner *v* show nonsupporting manner.
A. Defers to authority: supporting manner.
Assures Jack that his request will be considered. Is brief but warm and supporting. Avoids prolonged conversation. /1/
'Thank you Jack. We will check this with Mr. Land.'

117

'Would you mind checking this with Mr. Land?'

'Thank you Jack, I am sure Mr. Land will take care of it.'

B. Defers to Authority: nonsupporting Manner.   /1/

Refers Jack to Mr. Land but in a curt and rejecting manner.

'Go see Mr. Land will you?'

'I can't help you, Jack. That's Mr. Land's department.'

C. Establishes own rules: supporting manner.

Same as A, but:

    Alternatives.   /3/

    i. Asks for note.

    ii. Anticipates Mr. Land's decision.   /1/

       'I'm sorry to hear about that, Jack. We will arrange something else for you to do during recess period.'

D. Establishes own rules: nonsupporting manner.

Same as C, but is extremely abrupt or rejecting.

    Alternatives.

    i. Asks for note immediately.   /3/

       'Well, Jack, do you have a note?'

    ii. Orders Jack to his seat without reassuring him./1/

       'Go to your seat, Jack, the bell is about to ring.'

    iii. Dismisses the problem abruptly.

       'Don't bother me with this now.'

E. No response.

Feedback Descriptions (shown on right of page).

/1/ Jack nods and returns to his seat.

/3/ Jack reaches in his pocket and draws out a note.

PROBLEM ASSESSMENT

Stimulus Situation.

    1. Jack communicates to T that he has been sick the previous week.

    2. He asks for permission not to play during recess.

SUPPLEMENTARY INFORMATION

Jack is a low ability student who often receives criticism as a

118

personal attack. He has a tremendous desire to be loved, and cannot get enough attention.

This is the first item in Kersh's first 'in-basket'. The student will have read a description of the school and the community and also will have had a class orientation session. This is a tape-recording which describes various members of the class as they appear on slides. The supplementary information about Jack will have been given to the student in the orientation session.

During the exercise the student stands in front of the screen and the film begins to run. She is expected to recognize the cue, and react to it. Supposing that the student had not seen this as a situation that called for any response, then presumably the film would run on to the next problem. If the student does react, then her type of answer is recorded by the director, and the appropriate feedback sequence is originated. This is done by having film set up in four projectors: the feedback instructions (shown on right hand side of the page above) provide cues for the supervisor who switches on the appropriate projector, or, where the trainee's reaction has not been predicted, or where there is no filmed response, a verbal response is made. The supervisor records the student's response to each of the situations in a simple numerical code and these are permanently recorded.

An excellent aspect of this simulation is the follow up. When the trainee goes out on teaching practice subsequently a questionnaire is given to the supervising teacher. This contains seventeen questions which ask for his assessment on a five point scale under each of two headings: *frequency of technique* and *frequency of problem*. One of these questions is:

11. 'When direct action was required to control a disruptive group or individual, did the student-teacher act quickly as opposed to delay and allowing the disruption to spread?'

On the supervisor's response sheet it might have been answered thus:

	FREQUENCY OF TECHNIQUE					FREQUENCY OF PROBLEM				
	Always	*Often*	*Some-times*	*Seldom*	*Never*	*Very often*	*Often*	*Some-times*	*Seldom*	*Never*
1.										
2.										
3.										
–										
–										
11			X					X		

From this response it could be deduced that here was a teacher who had inadequate control, placed in a difficult class. These follow-up studies permit the effectiveness of the simulation as an instructional medium to be evaluated. The other potential use of simulation as a predictor of future performance could also be assessed by the use of this follow-up questionnaire. It is, of course, difficult to see how such a questionnaire could be used effectively in this country. If it was completed by the supervising tutor from the college of education, the probability is that the usual two visits a week would not be sufficient for him to make a realistic assessment. On the other hand the class teacher might be reluctant to make an accurate assessment of problem frequency if he felt there was an implied criticism of his class. On the whole the class teacher would probably be best fitted to make the assessment, subject to the above proviso.

Kersh asked 80 trainees the question 'How do you feel about your simulation experience?' and this drew 295 responses. Of these only one response said that it was generally not beneficial. This does not mean that all the rest of the responses were favourable. For example twelve replies said that they thought that the problems were unrealistic, and there were other critical responses which were fewer in number. Now, if 80 students were questioned and twelve thought that there was a lack of realism in the problems, or said so in response to an open-ended question, it would seem that in that sample 15 per cent was less than satisfied with the technique. This must be borne in mind, but its significance cannot be appreciated until there are comparable figures for other instructional techniques. Any lecturer might be delighted to learn that only 15 per cent of his audience was less than satisfied with one aspect of his lecture.

When he devised his simulation scheme, Kersh wanted to find a method by which his students could transfer their knowledge of teaching gained in the college to the classroom situation. He wanted to find a way of instructing teachers so that they would actually practise what they were taught. The original model for Kersh's simulations was the operant conditioning model. It was assumed that students had previously acquired highly differentiated ways of behaving in a classroom and that these became obvious during teaching practice. As a result of this, it was believed that the knowledge that they had gained from text books, lectures, and observations of model lessons was not shown when they were themselves in front of a class. It was further assumed that the behaviour of a teacher was shaped by situations that arose in the classroom, and that changes in a teacher's methods of instructing were dependent on the reinforcement he received consequent to his attempts to change. If this was so, it was argued that it was in the actual classroom that the tutor could best change the habits of his students.

There was, of course, a two-fold difficulty attached to this. In the first place it was difficult in America, as it is here, to get enough places for students. In the second place, having got into a classroom, there would then be no guarantee that the right stimuli could be produced at the times they were required. Thus the first task was to devise a situation that approximated to the real life situation, and the simulated classroom was considered to fill this role. It was then argued that the tutor could reinforce approximations to acceptable behaviour by making the 'pupils' in the simulated situation react positively towards it. If the student's behaviour was not acceptable, then the tutor could have the 'pupils' react negatively towards it. Of course this was a large order, and in practice it was not found possible to build the complete operant conditioning model. A change was made: instead of using

I

121

feedback to reinforce student behaviour, the newer technique uses feedback merely to inform students of the possible consequences of their behaviour, and it may or may not reinforce or control the student's subsequent behaviour. The latest research in the project is concerned with physical variables such as the image size on the screen.

Donald R. Cruickshank [1] of the University of Tennessee, with Frank W. Broadbent and Roy Bubb of the State University College, Brockport, New York, has devised a simulation training programme for student teachers. The unit is called the *Teaching Problems Laboratory*, and is intended to give student teachers a chance to make decisions in a lifelike classroom environment. A fictitious school district called 'Madison' has been created. Each participant in turn has to assume the role of Pat Taylor, a first year teacher of the fifth grade class at Longacre Elementary School (the choice of the name Pat is a deliberate one so that the role can be played by either men or women). Each participant is introduced to the community, the school district and the school by means of two film strips, 'Spotlight on Education in Madison', and 'Welcome to Longacre'. Pat Taylor also receives progress cards, sociograms and reading progress cards for thirty-one children, seventeen boys and fourteen girls; and also things less familiar to us here, such as faculty handbooks, course of study, and AV manuals.

There are thirty-one teaching problems in the exercise including those of student behaviour, parental relationships with the school, curriculum planning, teacher method, classroom management, and evaluation of learning. It is not suggested by the designers of the simulation that there are single correct answers to the problems, but the written answers given by students form a focus for discussion. The problems which make up the in-basket are presented in written incidents, on film and by means of role-playing. The materials are available for sale to colleges and other institutions. The Teaching Problems Laboratory contains two units, an Institutional Unit designed for the agency conducting the training programme, and a Participant's Unit containing those things that Pat Taylor has already been stated to have. The Institutional

Unit contains the two film strips and a gramophone record that goes with them and on which the 'superintendent' and the 'school principal' introduce the community and the school. Apart from this they contain the film, role-playing cards and written problems which make up the in-basket and finally a Participant's Unit.

Cruickshank has listed several advantages which he feels simulation techniques have over traditional methods in the education of teachers. As in Britain, there is the lack of opportunity for pre-service practice for trainee teachers. This is due both to the lack of places and to the distance from some colleges to teaching centres. He also sees significance in the fact that simulation exercises face students with problems earlier than they would normally meet them and more frequently. They can be given problems in the course of their training that they might not normally meet for a long time. The fact that they have once met them, and have had a chance of handling them without fear of criticism (or worse) for mistakes make them confident in the event of their arising during actual classroom occupancy.

A great value that decision making has is the value of discrimination. If one is free to choose and there are consequences of the decision, there is a value to be placed on discriminatory choice and the method of simulation gives important practice in decision making. Then there is the specific aspect of simulation: simulated case studies enable trainees to realize that children are individuals. To this extent the lessons learned in general in lectures and seminars about children are related to specific children by simulation, and there should be a carry over into on-the-job teaching practice at an earlier stage than might have been possible without simulation. The person who dives off the high board had first to learn how to jump into the swimming pool. So also the person who has learned by simulation how to manage problems in a classroom has then only to concentrate on content and so is more confident of his ability to handle a class than others who have not had the experience of simulation might be.

Teacher training simulation is being carried out at the

Indiana University School of Education. Here, however, those who administer feel that they have a duty to their students to make them familiar with a wide range of pupils. They have decided that their students on teaching practice might not see the over-intelligent or the very backward groups of pupils that the schools have great difficulty in handling adequately. There are other problem groups as well, such as the non-white, those with police records, those from poor homes opposed to education, and the recently arrived immigrants. Unlike other groups, the Indiana University *Insite* Project has taken a set of thirty-five actual records, photocopied them and then edited them to protect the pupils' identities. From these a final set of twenty-five folders was selected and these were used in the simulation exercise. Even though the name simulation is given to this project, the examples they quote savour more of the case-study and miss the point of involvement which seems so much a part of simulation. For instance, McQuigg [4] quotes '. . . Specific instances wherein interactions between the teacher and the student are suggested for possible role playing. For example: "In Jim's case, how might you deal with his mimicking you in class?" (Jim is an immature boy, rejected by his father, who receives little or no attention at home and is seeking to call attention to himself at school.)'

This item has two obvious faults. What teacher is liable to know that Jim, a quiet boy, has been rejected by his father or that he receives little or no attention at home? What teacher can find time in between collecting dinner money, handing out hymn books, doing dinner duty and playground supervision, and handling the other thirty-five to say to himself, 'Jim is an immature boy, rejected by his father, who receives little or no attention at home and is seeking to call attention to himself at school', between noticing that he is being mimicked and clouting Jim, who is an immature boy who receives little, etc., etc. The second point is that the whole thing about simulation is that *you are*, not *what would you do if*: involvement is the keynote. The *Inside* Project may have some good points but it is hardly simulation.

There are certain problems that concern those of us working

with simulation in the training of teachers. One of these is the relationship of realism to involvement and to effectiveness. Again and again we read that the closer we get to the real classroom situation the more effective will the transfer of training be. We have not found this to be the case: we have found rather that the simulation itself is the means of arousing interest, the conditioner, the basis on which discussion can be mounted. As Kersh found, it is not generally possible to use simulation exercises as reinforcers of approved behaviour, partly because there is no certainty that any teacher behaviour is necessarily the correct behaviour. Another reason that simulation cannot be used as a conditioner is that where a behaviour situation has a possibility of say four different actions, each of these actions may have say four separate consequences (that is, not everyone reacts in the same way to a given situation), and so the conditioning model rapidly becomes so complex that even a computer would have trouble handling it.

As colleges reach their maximum size, the already over-burdened schools will come under even heavier demands for teaching practice places. Almost certainly alterations in the form and style of teaching practice will have to be made. One way in which this might be done is to have longer practices, another is to group students in each class, but it surely must be considered as a possibility that students might be partly prepared by means of simulation exercises before they go out to do a reduced teaching practice. We have seen some few students who have been so prepared and feel that those who were able to handle the exercise gained in confidence when they faced their classes.

BIBLIOGRAPHY

1. CRUICKSHANK, DONALD B.: *Simulation: New Direction in Teacher Preparation.* Phi Delta Kappan, 48, Sept. 1966, 23–24.
2. JACOBS, ARTHUR J.: *Sociodrama and Teacher Education.* Journal of Teacher Education, 1, 1950, 193–8.

3. KERSH, BERT Y.: *Classroom Simulation: Further Studies on Dimensions of Realism, Appendices to Final Reports*. Title VII Project Number 5–0848, Oregon State System of Higher Education, Dec. 1965.
4. MCQUIGG, R. BRUCE: *Micro Groups Studied via Simulation*. Insite Project, School of Education, Indiana University, Undated. Mimeo.

RELATED READING

CRUICKSHANK, DONALD R.: *The Longacre School: A Simulated Laboratory for the Study of Teaching*. A paper prepared for the AACTE Workshop in Teacher Education, 1967. Mimeo.

CRUICKSHANK, DONALD R.: *Simulation: A Promising Technique for Improving Teacher Education*. University of Tennessee, Nashville, Undated. Mimeo.

CRUICKSHANK, DONALD R.: *21 Questions and Answers about the Teaching Problems Laboratory*. College of Education, University of Tennessee, Undated. Mimeo.

HERSHEY, GERALD L., KRUMBOLTZ, JOHN D. *and* SHEPARD, LORRAINE V.: *Effectiveness of Classroom Observation and Simulated Teaching in an Introductory Educational Psychology Course*. Journal of Educational Research, 58, Jan. 1965, 233–6.

KERSH, BERT Y.: *The Classroom Simulator*. Journal of Teacher Education, 13, Mar. 1962, 110–11.

MCQUIGG, R. BRUCE: *The Capstone Experience*. INSITE Project, School of Education, Indiana University, Undated. Mimeo.

SHARP, BERT L. *and* MAYER, W. K.: *Videotapes in Simulated Experiences and Supervision in Counselor Education*. In Television and Related Media. H. E. Bosley and H. E. Wigren (Eds.), Baltimore, Maryland, Multi-State Teacher Education Project, August 1967, 32–34.

TANSEY, P. J. *and* UNWIN, DERICK: *Simulation and Academic Gaming: Highly Motivational Teaching Techniques*. In Aspects of Educational Technology II. W. R. Dunn and C. Holroyd (Eds.), London, Methuen, 1969.

TWELKER, PAUL A.: *Classroom Simulation and Teacher Preparation*. 'School Review', 75, Summer 1967, 197–204.

WYNN, RICHARD: *Simulation: Terrible Reality in the Preparation of School Administrators*. Phi Delta Kappan, 46, December 1964, 170–3.

CHAPTER EIGHT

Computers and simulation

There are several situations in which simulation is used as a method of instruction in conjunction with computers. Where the skill to be taught is both complex and dangerous, the computer is an invaluable aid. Simulating flight conditions so that pilots can be trained in safety is too complex an operation to be undertaken without electronic aids. The computer permits an infinite variety of conditions to be set up, and it also allows reactions to the trainee's actions to be known almost instantaneously. The simulation of complex operations which cannot be broken down into simple parts or into many skills that can be learned individually needs the computer as an essential and integral part of the simulation.

In business education the computer is frequently used with simulations. Often it is not an essential part of these exercises, but is used as an aid to simplify the work of the umpire, to extend the number of choices of action, or to increase the complexity of the mathematical model on which the game is based. There are complex business games that could not function unless a computer was used with them, but even these do not make the computer an essential element in business education. In business education one may analyse the skills that are required for competence, and these skills can then be taught separately using simple games, or they can be taught together. If they are taught together, then the game may very well become a complex one in which the use of a computer is necessary.

The difference between business training and training in such complex concept and motor skills as those required by pilots is that the former skills can be learned 'end on', while the latter cannot. The pilot needs to master a great variety of skills which he has to use at the same time, and he cannot function unless he has learned all of the skills, even as a trainee. The simulation required for a pilot's training is *essentially* complex, whereas that used in business is *optionally* complex. ERGOM [7] games are examples of business games which teach one of the skills of industry and business at a time and which, consequently, do not need computers for their successful operation. Patently, if these skills can be taught in this way, then other essential skills can also be so taught.

It is doubtful whether computers will be used in simulation in formal classroom education in this country for some time. It is not even certain that they have a place in the classroom type of simulation, because one of the advantages of simulation as a teaching aid is that its simplicity permits its individual use by different teachers in ways that each has found best for himself. Computer-based simulations take away this privilege and make the simulations stereotyped and universally applicable. It is true, of course, that computers have been used in the classroom at many different levels of formal education, from early secondary-school age to postgraduate university training. What is not so certain is that their use was either necessary or even beneficial, in these situations. Instances of their use will be given from time to time in this chapter, and the reader will then be free to form his own conclusions.

The section of education which has used computers the most is probably that of the social sciences. The part of the social sciences which has been simulated the most is the area of international relationships. This is logical in this time of wars,

128

both hot and cold. If we care for those we teach, we should surely make them aware of the world in which they live, and of the processes of decision making that take place in that world. Further, by using simulation, we put the participants in such a position that they have to make decisions. By this means it is hoped that they will become more acutely aware of international relationships and will be rather more than passive observers.

The first, and best known, of these international type simulations was devised by Professor Harold Guetzkow [9] of Northwestern University. Subsequently a great deal of research has been carried out in his department, and a typical simulation which uses computers has been developed and produced by Paul Smoker [14]. His aim is to give participants a variety of experiences which they use to make decisions in a simplified version of the international world. His world is made up of model nations and international organizations which engage in diplomatic activities and trade negotiations. The simulation covers a period of about twenty years and is played out over two days. It is broken down into hour periods each of which represents a year.

At the beginning of each period the director of the simulation gives each country information on its economic and defence positions and on its type of government. The corporations are also told about costs, production and distribution, and about their inventory. In this simulation, it is claimed that the use of a limited amount of computer programming has permitted a greater complexity to be introduced, and a tendency to make it, as a consequence, closer to the reality of decision making in the real world. One hundred and twenty-four variables are used in this simulation, and there is a very complex variety of relationships between them.

An advantage of the use of the computer in this sort of simulation, it is claimed, is that it can give immediate feedback. In the manual form of simulation, the end of a period is looked on as the time at which the participant is told how his simulated environment has responded to his previous decisions. If, as is the case in Smoker's simulation, 'on-line' computing

129

facilities are used, then it is possible to have a continuous feedback of information.

Smoker (15, Appendix A2) states that participants find the following advantages associated with simulation.

'1. They achieved a feel for the world as government officials experience it.

2. They found simulation easier to grasp than the remote and complicated international situation that they read about in text books and the news media.

3. They gained the ability to understand important components of the international community by analysing similar components in the model.'

It seems that the third of these advantages is a justification for the use of computers in such simulations when they are used at university level. If the structure of the international community is to be studied in a simplified form using simulation, then, as long as it is easy to understand, the more complex and close to reality the simulation is, the better. The computer not only provides this complexity, but its continuous feedback also gives the participant immediate reinforcement. While not essential to simulation of social sciences, the computer can be beneficial in so far as it is used to give an air of reality to the proceedings.

It has been used at a much earlier age, and at a much less sophisticated level, in the study of economics. Wing [4] and Moncreiff [5] have devised a computer-based model of the ancient Sumerian society in order to teach basic economics to sixth-grade (twelve-year-old) children. These children, who are pupils at Mohansic School in the Yorktown Heights district of New York, have to assume the role of a ruler in this ancient pre-Greek civilization. The simulation is played in isolation. The player sits at a console and plays the game out against the computer which has the simulation model in its information store. The pupil, during the game, has to make decisions in such a way that his simulated Sumerian state survives a series of crises, both political and natural. It is hoped that in the solving of these problems the pupil will have learned to understand the processes that are at work in a developing

130

civilization, and that he will have developed the ability to make decisions while realizing that there are conflicting values and goals involved in these decisions.

Two further games were developed, and Wing [4] (pp. 3 and 4) has published his findings. He found that the children who could read had no difficulty in playing the games with only minimal assistance from the supervisor. The game lasted for fifteen hours, and, with one exception, the children were highly motivated. As Wing points out, working with computers was a novel experience, and he does not know whether interest would be maintained for a long time. As far as method effectiveness is concerned, Wing's findings were that in the Sumerian game his experimental group gained more from pre-test to post-test than did his control group, and this gain was statistically significant at the 1 per cent level. There was a considerable saving of teaching time. A further advantage of, and justification for, the use of computers in this series of games is that it makes possible some form of individualizing of instruction. In this sense the computer is performing the function of a teaching machine with a branching programme. In the published work about this series of games nothing specific is said about the economic concepts that it is hoped to teach. It is difficult under these circumstances to see what contribution the computer makes, and whether or not it is sledgehammer used to crack a nut.

Coleman [6] considers computers to have a vital part to play in research in the social sciences. Without the computer, he says, the dependent variable when we are analysing data is the individual. With it, we can turn away from the behaviour of the individual and look at the behaviour of the system itself. When the computer is used, research tends to be along the lines of the anthropologist's building up the few clues he possesses in order to 'recreate a functioning community', rather than the analysis of the survey researcher when he investigates why people change jobs. In Coleman's view, the computer makes possible a synthesis where only the possibility of analysis exists without it. He quotes specific examples in this paper of its use in clique determination, reference-group phenomena, stability and instability of groups, and mentions McPhee and Smith's [7] work in simulating a voting system.

Abt [8] has reviewed the characteristics of computer simulations of social, political and economic models (p. 54). These simulations are usually done on general-purpose, high-speed, digital computers. Because the latter calculate at such high speeds, computer-based simulations of extremely complex systems take little calculation time. He says that computer simulation is particularly effective when the model is expressed in quantitative or logical relationships. When the processes of the simulation are complex and the various parts of the model have an exact or precise relationship, computer-based simulation is particularly effective. Coleman, in his survey, found this almost universally applicable to economic models, and, consequently, most economic models either have or intend to use computer simulations.

Social and political models, Coleman says, can be equally complex, but the integral parts lack the clearly defined inter-relationship common in the economic models. As a result such games are frequently manual as opposed to computer-based. This is true of Smoker's International Processes Simulation mentioned earlier. This has been kept as a man-machine game so that changes in the model can more readily be made as the inter-relationships between the various parts of the model become clearer; and indeed, in order that the model may be easily modified in the light of operational experience.

Smoker [9] in another work compares manual and machine simulations. In manual simulation he sees a basic understanding of underlying principles without an understanding of how the process works. Here there are no explicit, predetermined criteria, and decision is left to human judgement. Because of this last fact, such games usually require an umpire whose function is to make independent judgements of feasibility and in general to make both decisions and evaluations. With computer-based simulations he associates the absence of human value judgements and the universality of prediction. No umpire is required, and he sees their value primarily as a research tool. He says (p. 6) . . . 'The type of situation modelled is one where the facts are fairly well known and can be matched with explicit criteria.' In man-computer simulations he sees the function of the computer as being similar to that of the umpire in manual simulations. It imposes constraints on the human value judgements.

What starts out as a research simulation is frequently used afterwards as a teaching tool. From one such simulation, other second- and third-generation simulations of greater complexity can be built. The previously mentioned Inter-Nation Simulation by Guetzgow is an example of a first-generation simulation that has been used in this way. There are versions of it that have been simplified for use in schools. Smoker's own simulation, based on it, is a second-generation simulation of increased complexity, and probably further refining will be done in order that a more involved simulation can be derived from the International Processes simulation.

When used as research tools, simulations take a long time to develop, for there is a constant effort to achieve perfection, or to make the model as close to the reality as it is possible to do. Ultimately, and if the simulation is computer-based, it should be possible to use it as a forecaster of future performance. If a model is developed, and if known phenomena can be derived exactly and precisely and consistently by using the simulation, then it is a logical consequence that the simulation can be used to see into the future. It is true that this has not so far been possible, but until now computers have been relatively unsophisticated instruments compared with the human brain. At some future time, given the increased sophistication of computers that we can reasonably expect, the development and refinement of simulations based on previous experience, and the ability to refine models continuously, this should be an important new use for simulation techniques. Already attempts are being made to use them in a number of branches of research such as the behavioural sciences and in educational data processing.

In the behavioural sciences many workers are aware of the values of digital computers, but few use them. This is possibly because of the inter-disciplinary demarcation lines. The average behavioural scientist does not understand the technical language of the computer scientist, his method of programming information, or the part played by the computer in research. Baker [10] describes a course to improve the knowledge of behavioural scientists. It is conducted over a semester at the University of Wisconsin, and an outline of the course is given in his paper. Its aim is to produce a research worker who can communicate his needs to the professional programmer, can use existing programmes, and can make an appraisal of his needs in terms of programming.

An excellent description of the development of a theory of problem-solving is provided by Newell, Shaw and Simon [11]. In this paper they develop the elements of a theory of human problem solving, and attempt to provide evidence of validity. In their conclusion (pp. 165–166) they extend their theory to the implications of this approach to the study of general information-processing theory. When the behaviour of a system is described by a well specified programme defined in terms of elementary processes, they compare the programme's role with that of a system of differential equations in a classical applied-mathematics problem.

They describe the uses made of such programmes, namely their use to deduce general properties of the system, their use to predict behaviour, which predictions can then be compared with actual behaviour observed in experiment, and finally their modification when their predictions do not fit the observed facts. It is claimed that digital computers have two main advantages as far as such programming is concerned. First, they permit us to determine the behaviour implied by a programme under a variety of environmental conditions. Second, because programmes are specific and so free us from the vagueness of theories normally associated with higher mental processes, they permit us to see if the processes are possible and if they are sufficient to explain the phenomena.

An easily readable extension of the work in the behavioural sciences is reported by Howland and Hunt [12]. They were aware of the excellent work of Newell, Shaw and Simon, and using this as a starting point they developed a series of models for human concept formation. They found that their model had features that differed from those of human concept learners and required modification. For instance, the computer had unlimited memory storage while humans do not. It can handle only relatively simple, conjunctive concepts, whereas humans can handle . . . 'multidimensional, relational, and perhaps disjunctive concepts'. Lastly their model had no preference for answers that make use of particularly significant information.

In the autumn of 1960 at the University of California, Berkley, Feigenbaum [13] conducted a course in computer simulation of cognitive processes. Five units of research were carried out by students on this course and are reported in *Behavioral Science*. The papers by Wickelgren [14] and Allen [15] used Bruner, Goodnow and Austin's book *A Study of Thinking* as a starting point from which to develop studies in concept attainment. Wickelgren sets out to devise a programme such that concepts can be discovered by the computer when cards, some of which are exemplars of the concept and some of which are not, are presented to it. He outlines the kind of memory structure on which his concept-attainment model is built and points to parts that need modification. It is a brief paper which shows that the state of the art of computer simulation is still primitive, but it offers hope for the future.

Teaching is part art and part science. It is part art because we do not know what makes a person learn. Each of us can remember some particular item from our schooldays, often not fixed in time or place to the overall learning situation. If we knew what enabled us to learn and to remember that particular piece of information, teaching would cease to be an art and would be wholly a science. If it is possible to simulate the higher cognitive processes by computer, and then to refine the simulations and continuously to modify the models, then it might enable us to make teaching a science. This would be a positive step towards extending the limits of educability.

There are practical aspects of classroom and school organization where simulation is beginning to be practised as a by-product of educational data processing. Education in our society is an extremely costly business, and, considered from an efficiency point of view, is not very efficient. The first of the limits placed on formal education is imposed by the timetable. Many schools are unable to offer courses because they are restricted by timetables. Timetables and whole school systems can be simulated and investigated by computers. It is being done at the present time and will continue to be important. People tend to categorize data and deal with each of the categories individually. This results in a loss of perspective of the system as a whole. At present, educational data processing depends on the master schedule or organizational set-up. As this is prepared manually and is not subjected to rigid logic checks, there is no guarantee that it is the most effective in any case.

An entire educational system is extremely complex, but, with the digital computer, the means of simulating it are to hand. Also to hand are the methods of studying, manipulating and modifying the system. On the other hand, such simulations are expensive, and they present problems of reliability, of validity, and of proximation to the original, that must be taken into account. Some models of school systems have been developed in America, and the papers by Wurtele [16] and by Cogswell, *et al* [17], are of interest in this relatively recent area of development. Other areas of organization that have been simulated are the design of school bus routes, siting and design of school classrooms, and design versus cost estimates for school buildings. Schools can make the wisest decisions only when they have the fullest information and when this information is broad in scope. It is possible that simulation may be a source of supply for such information.

An obvious necessity when a computer is used for simulation is to communicate the problem to the machine. This process has been considerably aided by the design of special-purpose programmes including higher-level languages. These languages and the 'software packages' that implement them permit the programmer to write his programme and communicate it to the machine without having to do so in machine language. The number of languages and packages has increased rapidly and frequently more than one is available for any given job. In this case the operator must choose which one he will use. Information and bibliographies that might be of assistance in this are available in Teichroew and Lubin's book [16], and a useful simulation language, IPL-V, is described by Baker and Martin [14].

To conclude, it has been indicated that there is a need for computers in simulation at present where the skills to be learned are complex and the risks involved in training are great. They are also of use when the equipment used in connection with the dangerous training is expensive. A further use is in research, especially in the behavioural sciences and into the more complex cognitive processes. At present computer-based simulation is expensive and only marginally available. It is doubtful if it is worth the expense at the classroom level, especially as here it is best if the teacher together with the children design their own simulations. But what is unusual today becomes the commonplace of tomorrow. How many of us envisaged the overwhelming use of television receivers in schools as short a time as ten years ago? It could well be that the computer will become the programmed-learning machine of the future with all of the status that these machines never had. When this happens, simulation, which is one way to programme instruction, may well be computer based in every school.

BIBLIOGRAPHY

1. ERGOM : *European Research Group on Management.* Rue de la Concorde, 53, Bruxelles V, Belgium.
2. GUETZKOW, HAROLD, ALGER, C., BRODY, R., NOEL, R. and SNYDER, R.: *International Relations: Developments for Research and Teaching.* Prentice Hall Inc., Englewood Cliffs, New Jersey, 1963.
3. SMOKER, PAUL: *International Process Simulation: A Man-Computer Model.* Evanston, Illinois, Northwestern University, 1968.
4. WING, RICHARD L.: *A Report of an Experiment with Computer-based Economic Games.* A paper prepared for the Annual Meeting of the AERA, 16 Feb., 1967.
5. MONCREIFF, BRUCE: *The 'Sumerian Game': Teaching Economics*

With a Computerized P.I. Program. Programmed Instruction, 4, 1965, pp. 10–11.

6. COLEMAN, JAMES S.: *Analysis of Social Structures and Simulation of Social Processes With Electronic Computers.* Educational and Psychological Measurement, XXI (1), 1961, pp. 203–18.

7. MCPHEE, W. N. *and* SMITH, R.: *A Model for Analysing Voting Systems.* Bureau of Applied Social Research, Columbia University, 1960.

8. ABT ASSOCIATES INC.: *Survey of the State of the Art: Social, Political, and Economic Models and Simulations.* Cambridge, Mass., 26 Nov., 1965.

9. SMOKER, PAUL *and* MARTIN, J.: *Modern Trends in Education: Simulation and Games: An Overview.* Chicago, S.R.A., Unit, 8, 15 May, 1968.

10. BAKER, FRANK B.: *A Computer Course for the Behavioral Scientist.* Educational and Psychological Measurement, Vol. XXII, 3, 1962, pp. 617–21.

11. NEWELL, ALLEN, SHAW, J. C. *and* SIMON, HERBERT A.: *Elements of a Theory of Human Problem Solving.* Psychological Review, 65 (3), 1958, pp. 151–66.

12. HOWLAND, CARL I. *and* HUNT, EARL B.: *Computer Simulation of Concept Attainment.* Behavioral Science, 5, 1960, pp. 265–7.

13. FEIGENBAUM, EDWARD A.: *An Experimental Course in Simulation of Cognitive Processes.* Behavioral Science, 7, 1962, pp. 244–5.

14. WICKELGREN, WAYNE A.: *A Simulation Program for Concept Attainment by Conservative Focusing.* Behavioral Science, 7, 1962, pp. 245–7.

15. ALLEN, MAX: *A Concept Attainment Program that Simulates a Simultaneous-Scanning Strategy.* Behavioral Science, 7, 1962, pp. 247–50.

16. WURTELE, ZIVIA S.: *Mathematical Models for Educational Planning.* SP–3015, California, Systems Development Corp., 30 Nov., 1967.

17. COGSWELL, JOHN F., BRATTEN, J. E., EGBERT, R. E., ESTAVAN, D. P., MARSH, D. G. *and* YETT, F. A.: *Analysis of Instructional Systems.* SDC Document TM–1493/201/00, Apr. 1966.

18. TEICHROEW, DANIEL *and* LUBIN, JOHN FRANCIS: *Computer Simulation – Discussion of the Technique and Comparison of Languages.* Communications of the ACM, 9 (10), Oct. 1966, pp. 723–40.

19. BAKER, FRANK B. *and* MARTIN, THOS. J.: *An IPL-V Technique for Simulation Programs.* Educational and Psychological Measurement, XXV (3), 1965, pp. 859–65.

RELATED READING

ARMITAGE, PETER *and* SMITH, CYRIL: *The Development of Computable Models of the British Educational System and their Possible Uses.* Mathematical Models in Educational Planning, OEDC, Paris, 1967.

COGSWELL, J. F., EGBERT, R. L., MARSH, D. G. *and* YETT, F. A.: *New Solutions to Implementing Instructional Media Through Analysis and Simulation of School Organization.* SDC Document TM–1809, 24 Mar., 1964.

COLEMAN, J. S.: *The Use of Electronic Computers in the Study of Social Organization.* European Journal of Sociology, VI, 1965, pp. 89–107.

INGHAM, GEORGE E.: *Simulated Environments For Individual Instruction.* Audiovisual Instruction, 9 Sept., 1964, pp. 410–11.

INGRAHAM, LEONARD W.: *Teachers, Computers, and Games: Innovations in the Social Studies.* Social Education, 31 Jan., 1967, pp. 51–53.

MAJAK, R. ROGER: *Social Science Teaching with Inter-Nation Simulation: A Review.* Social Studies, LIX (3), Mar. 1968, pp. 116–19.

SMOKER, PAUL: *Analysis of Conflict Behaviours in an International Process Simulation and an International System.* Evanston, Ill., Northwestern University, Aug. 1968.

UNWIN, DERICK *and* ATKINSON, FRANK: *The Computer in Education.* The Library Association London, 1968.

WING, RICHARD L.: *Computer Controlled Economics Games for the Elementary School.* Audiovisual Instruction, 9 Dec., 1964, pp. 681–2.

YASAKI, Ed.: *Educational Data Processing.* Datamation, 9 June, 1963, pp. 24–27.

CHAPTER NINE

Endpiece

This book has been written because the authors have used simulation techniques and have found them to be satisfying methods both in teacher training and in the classroom. It has covered a wide field because little had been written in book form before, and because written material is difficult to obtain. For this reason we felt the need to cover a wide range of simulation activities, and to put a bibliography and a reading list at the end of each chapter. By doing this, we hoped that those of our readers who became interested would have a starting point from which to read further for themselves. The references we have quoted are available in Great Britain, and can be obtained if your librarians are as co-operative as are those in the Reading University Education library.

At the same time, because we believe that the method is a good one with many advantages, we feel that it will have the greatest impact if teachers see that it has advantages. The ordinary classroom teacher has little time to get to a library, less money to spend on photocopying at sixpence a sheet for material that might help, and with the least opportunity of anyone concerned with education to spend time on experimenting. For this reason, we propose now to end the book with an example of the use of simulation by a practising teacher in a comprehensive school.

The class was a third-year group which had been streamed and which was classified as 'C'. In other words it was the bottom of the year range except for the remedial group. The simulation was a co-operative effort by the teacher and the whole class, and the teacher's only experience of simulation was observation of a simulation carried out by one of the authors, and frequent talks about it.

The scene was set in the first session thus: . . . Marston is a small village about six miles from the large town of Craysmere. It has a pub called the Miller of Tyre, two general stores, one of which is the local sub-post-office run by Mrs Leedham, the other selling newspapers, wool and general hardware as well as being an average corner store. It is run by Mr George Harris. There is a village hall which is in use on Monday, Wednesday and Saturday nights each week for village meetings including those of the parish council, and such entertainments as bingo and card games such as whist. The village has a doctor who has been there for only six months. He is fairly young and it is his first practice. There is a population of some one hundred between the ages of eleven and eighteen years.

While it is a quiet village, with the last bus out of the place at seven thirty at night and no more in until seven in the morning, it has a local policeman, P.C. Grey, who has foregone promotion and has been in the village for twelve years. He is well liked. His rule of the village has been in the old-fashioned way. If a child misbehaved, he would either box his ears or tell his father, who would do it harder. He had not arrested anybody until three of the village youths broke into Mrs Leedham's store. They did not steal anything because the noise woke Mrs Leedham, who came downstairs, put the light on and recognized Tommy Cook, a fifteen-year-old who worked for her part-time while he attended the grammar school at Craysmere. She rang the local policeman, who had to take action. He managed to find the culprits, had to charge them, and they were put on probation in the juvenile court. Mr

Thomas Cook, the father of the grammar-school boy, had said in court that this would never have happened if there had been some sort of activity in the village in which the youth could participate.

There is no secondary school in the village; the children have to go to Craysmere either to the grammar school or to one of the secondary modern schools. The primary school is run by Mr Tasker, who has been headmaster for three years. He is forty-seven years old and does not understand the needs of older children, believing that they should have enough to occupy their time in the evenings with their homework.

The village is really a two-part one. On the one hand, many of the families are old-established and owe some sort of allegiance to the squire, Major Thomson, who owns the Glebe Farm. This is a mixed farm of a thousand acres and employs a large number of men. But apart from this, Major Thomson owns a number of cottages in the village, and so his opinions carry weight. He has one son of sixteen who goes to a public school, and does not have a high opinion of the local youth in general. He is a magistrate.

On the other hand, the village is within fifty miles of London and so is a dormitory town in the commuter belt. It is a pretty village with a number of fine old stone houses. About half of these middle-class people send their children to preparatory and public schools, but the rest are satisfied with the local primary and the Craysmere grammar schools.

There is a local church dating back, at least in part, to Saxon times. The vicar is a young man of thirty who is keen on youth and is anxious to help them. The break-in made him aware of the need for some form of organized entertainment for them in the evenings. He knows, and who better, that the devil finds work for idle hands. He has called a meeting of the village people during which he proposes to enlist their support for the starting of a youth club. He knows that the hall is free on three week nights and hopes, when he has enlisted support and gained approval for a youth club, to get the use of the hall for a peppercorn rental. There are difficulties, as he well knows there will be, but he hopes that the majority of

142

people will support his ideas of a youth club. On the night of the meeting the following people turn out. It will be interesting to see what conclusions they reach.

Name	Age	Occupation	In favour	Opposed	Un-certain
				ATTITUDE TO YOUTH CLUB	
Mrs Leedham	50	storekeeper		x	
George Harris	42	storekeeper			x
Dr Marger	29	doctor	x		
Mr Grey	37	policeman	x		
Mr Thos. Cook	45	commercial salesman	x		
Major Thomson	67	landowner		x	
Mr Tasker	47	headmaster			x
Mr Moore	38	smallholder			x
Rev Jenkins	30	vicar	x		
Mr Mason	51	publican	x		
Emma Mays	19	shop assistant			x
Mrs Green	33	housewife and parish councillor		x	
Mrs Thomson	59	housewife		x	

Other names could be added as required, depending on the number in the class. At this stage the teacher gave the class the opportunity to ask any further questions about the village, and then, having invented the answers, assigned roles to class members. In a large class two children could be assigned to each role.

As soon as the children had been given their roles they were required to write a description of the person, his background, the number of children in the family, and other information that would help to explain his feelings about youth and his

143

attitude towards the forming of a youth club. Each child then had to make this information available to the others, and after this the meeting began.

It was explained to the children, many of whom were reserved and diffident about talking publicly, that they were the character they were portraying, and, although they themselves would have little to say, the character would have a lot to say. For instance, Mrs Leedham, whose shop was broken into by a boy that she was employing, would have a lot to say about the trustworthiness of the youth of today.

The simulation, which has so far occupied six timetable periods has proved a firm favourite with the children, who have been both surprisingly articulate and involved. They are reluctant to leave the lessons. At this stage, a stormy meeting has agreed to the formation of a youth club. Work in moral education can proceed from this point by changing roles so that the class represents members of the youth club. Crisis situations such as vandalism, or theft by one of the members, or a discussion about the advisability of permitting the shop-breakers to join, can be developed. There are a great many possibilities.

Simulation is a new field for workers in education in this country. Little practical work has been done to date, but there is an increasing number of enthusiasts anxious to find out more about it and to experiment with it in the schools. Amongst the first users of simulation, if not the first, was Professor William Taylor who used in-basket techniques for the training of head-teachers. At the present time the following people are prominent in the various aspects of simulation in education. The Wiltshire Youth Organizer, Mr A. Aldrich, has used the method most effectively and for a long time in the training of youth leaders. Rex Walford of Maria Grey College, Twickenham, has designed a number of Geography games, and Tony Crisp has used them in the classroom and on a television programme. Two other workers in simulation in the field of social studies are W. Van der Eyken of the Department of of Education, Brunel University, and Robert Boardman of the University of Surrey, whose article in the *World and the*

School, number 14, October 1968, is very well set out and describes actual classroom work. Both of these people have worked with children and have either devised simulations or modified existing ones in international relations so that they are applicable to our educational situation. During the past year the authors have had over three hundred requests for information and help from a variety of places and a wide range of educators.

We are sure that simulation has a large number of applications and some features that could, with advantage, be incorporated into most classrooms. It is hoped, in the near future, to publish a variety of simulations which will serve as starting points for busy teachers to use both in the classrooms and as a basis for other simulations of their own.

Index

147

Index

Index

Index